AN EMERGENCY IN
SLOW MOTION

Handbook of Psychobiography (editor)
Tiny Terror: Why Truman Capote (Almost) Wrote Answered Prayers

AN EMERGENCY IN SLOW MOTION

The Inner Life of Diane Arbus

William Todd Schultz

BLOOMSBURY

New York   Berlin   London   Sydney

To Theresa

Published by Bloomsbury USA, New York

All papers used by Bloomsbury USA are natural, recyclable products made from wood grown in well-managed forests. The manufacturing processes conform to the environmental regulations of the country of origin.

LIBRARY OF CONGRESS CATALOGING-IN-PUBLICATION DATA

Schultz, William Todd.
An emergency in slow motion : the inner life of Diane Arbus / William Todd Schultz. — 1st U.S. ed.
p. cm.
Includes bibliographical references.
ISBN-13: 978-1-60819-519-0
ISBN-10: 1-60819-519-8
1. Arbus, Diane, 1923–1971—Psychology. 2. Photographers—United States—Biography. I. Title.
TR140.A73S38 2011
779.092—dc22
[B]
2010052420

First U.S. Edition 2011

1 3 5 7 9 10 8 6 4 2

Typeset by Westchester Book Group
Printed in the U.S.A. by Quad/Graphics, Fairfield, Pennsylvania

(William Gedney Photographs/Courtesy of Duke University)

CONTENTS

INTRODUCTION

THE PSYCHOLOGIST WILLIAM MCGUIRE, in a long essay on hypothesis generation in psychology—an unfortunately neglected subject—makes the following observation about the study of lives. It might be optimal, he suggests, to use cases "with intermediate puzzlingness, not so obvious to be devoid of new information and not so obscure as to be baffling."[1]

I have to confess. After six or seven years of trying to make sense of the photographer Diane Arbus—looking closely at her life, looking even more closely at her pictures—I still feel, in many ways and with varying degrees of vexation, somewhat baffled. Arbus is a mystery. To get the shots that made her name she went to the bottom of the night, as Auden once said of Yeats, and I followed her there, risked the descent, but a lot of the trip remains, even now, more or less unilluminated. But that's the thing about darkness. You can't shine a light to see it. The dark has to stay dark. You feel your way around, then crawl back out of it with whatever cargo you've managed to pinch. On this same subject Nabokov quotes King Lear: "To take upon us the mystery

1

of things: this is my suggestion for everyone who takes art seriously."[2]

There is an impulse in the study of artists to treat them as irreducibly unique, unreachably beyond the pale. Yes, art is a mystery, and Arbus is too. Yes, there is much about her and her work that can never be known. But we are all mysteries. Lives begin and end in mystery. What one works toward, and what I try to present in this book, are slipping glimpses of the mysterious X factor *why*, the elusive needs or motives or tendencies at the root of self-expression. What emerges is truth, but as direction, not destination, more a pathway than a location. We never know everything, but we don't know nothing.

There's only one biography of Diane Arbus, Patricia Bosworth's full-length study published in 1984. It is a brave, determined effort, written without the cooperation of an estate that tends to be inhospitable to even the most sincere and well-intentioned trespasses, and in many ways it succeeds. Facts are laid out. Several key figures are interviewed—Arbus's brother, the poet Howard Nemerov, and her mother, Gertrude Nemerov. A portrait forms. Arbus is a little bit less unknown. But in the twenty-six years since Bosworth, more has come to light. At long last the estate brought out its own contribution to the Arbus story, *Revelations*, with newly published pictures, an annotated timeline, and gingerly culled samplings from notebooks and letters. And more people have gone on record since 1984, talking about what it felt like to be photographed by Arbus—what she said to them and what she asked them to do, the impression she left. This is all in the nature of biography. New facts have a way of trickling out, confirming or challenging prior understandings. And as they accrete, as they start to add up, sometimes anomalously, new possibilities present themselves. The time arrives for an updated picture, a revision of past attempts at meaning making. Not all revisions are revolutionary, but in the best of instances, they add a few more form-creating pieces to the overall jigsaw, the life's gestalt.

This book is not a biography. My aim is not to present the life in all its fullness, from beginning to end. I deliberately leave stones unturned—some dull, some shiny. Instead, my intention is to make sense of Diane Arbus's *psychological* life—her goals, her dreams, her view of herself, her strategies, not all of them conscious, for dealing with difficult feelings, her modes of psychological defense, and most importantly the subjective origins of the pictures themselves, the art, the source of her fame. I interpret the pictures, in light of her life history, as self-expressions. The goal is to know better what she was after, what she was trying to say, whether she knew that clearly or not.

Analyses of lives that zero in on a person's psychology and, in order to do so, make use of psychological theory and research are usually called psychobiographies, a term of opprobrium for some. Bad psychobiographies exist. I've read them. I have no interest in defending them. In fact, I'm all for calling them bad when they are so. But the existence of bad psychobiography proves nothing about psychobiography in general, any more than bad dentistry proves anything about dentistry in general. Each instance rises or falls on its own merits. It works or it doesn't work. It persuades or it fails to persuade. Like most everything else in life, the proof is in the pudding. The fair, thoughtful reader will reach his or her own conclusion. There is no other possible arrangement, and it is one I'm perfectly comfortable with. Sources do exist about the meaning and practice of psychobiography, for those with more than passing interest. One is my own *Handbook of Psychobiography*, which I edited for Oxford University Press in 2005. Another is a book by Alan Elms, *Uncovering Lives: The Uneasy Alliance of Biography and Psychology*. Both take a sympathetic line, and both contain plenty of examples of psychobiographical essays that make good sense of extraordinary people, from George W. Bush to Elvis.

The fact that I take a psychological approach to Arbus's art is not meant to suggest I find that angle *sufficient* unto itself. The pictures might be examined purely artistically, with no biographical context at all. They might, in other words, simply be viewed—though such an engagement is never quite simple— and understood from the inside out, more or less intrinsically, like found objects. This appears to be the Arbus estate's recommendation, to take the shots as they are, unencumbered by any disfiguring life-history lens. The pictures might also be scrutinized in light of their historical comparables in photography, their milieu, their technical features. One might also connect them to other studies of so-called grotesques, photographic or literary. The possibilities are endless. My belief, however, is that in Arbus's case especially—where photography is referred to as a "private sin," where pictures are called "secrets about a secret," to cite only two asides by the artist herself—a psychological posture is *necessary*: not sufficient, but necessary. Knowing what Arbus was trying to get out, and why, lends power and poignancy to the images. It's an addition, not a subtraction.

My orienting assumption, then, which I work to defend with facts and interpretations, is this: Arbus's art revealed her in ways even she may not have grasped, and her method, her technique, her choice of a particular subject or individual print, and her thoughts on the purpose and meaning of photography all express personal and sometimes intimate, concealed truths. As would be true of any artist, the art is largely—fractionally—covert autobiography. I aim to make the covert overt. I superimpose the life on Arbus's art to better understand the art, and vice versa.

Art is always part pure expression, a consciously managed attempt to say something that's important to the person making it. It is what the artist intends it to be; it means what she wants it to mean. Arbus took the shots she did because she was Diane Arbus. The uniqueness of her vision was clear to her: "I do feel I have some slight corner on something about the quality of things. I mean it's very subtle and a little embarrassing to me, but I really believe there are things which nobody would see unless I photographed them."[3]

But art is also often *defensive*, an unconsciously driven effort to say or show things without knowing what's being said or shown. It is *more* than the person intends it to be; it means *more* than she wants it to mean. Artists aren't always in complete command of their material. Sometimes it commands them and they let it; they get out of the way, the subject matter comes unbidden, it compels them and they follow its lead. In this case what's needed is deep interpretation. Going beyond what's simply there. Getting at the subtext. Uncovering what's latent, what's driving the more manifest content.

But how does one do such a thing? By making informed, careful, illuminating use of solid psychological theory and research and, in a sense, aiming it at the art and the life to see what it exposes. Now, in Arbus's case, as in most others, the biography points in certain theoretical directions. If we keep an open mind, refrain from preselecting particular theoretical angles, the facts of the life can lead us to our choices. In a word, it's usually best to entertain a flexible *eclecticism*.

Arbus's early life was lonely and difficult; she was raised not by her parents but a series of governesses, almost all of whom she disliked; she talks about feeling loathsome and humiliated; her mother, often depressed and cut off, felt unloving; her father, whom Arbus calls a phony, always putting on a front, was unreachably away at work. "The world seemed to me to belong to the world," she says, and what she learned "never seemed to be my own experience."[4] Throughout her life Arbus craved intimacy, sought relationships compulsively, feared rejection. All these indicators suggest an approach based on attachment, a scientifically validated model focusing on the surprisingly wide-ranging behavioral and emotional sequelae of formative relationships. To adequately understand Arbus it's essential to explore her early years, feelings she references such as shame and sadness, the means or attachment-related strategies she relied on to get her needs met, and how all these dynamics and processes together gave rise to a particular personality organization that in some ways prefigured the art.

A lot of Arbus's relationships have been called symbiotic. That is in fact the theme, or one theme, of the Patricia Bosworth biography. Arbus's relationship with Doon, her first daughter, was symbiotically close; so was her relationship with her husband, Allan Arbus, whom she met and instantly fell in love with at age fourteen. Arbus didn't just get close to people; she got desperately close. She lost and found herself in others, including her photographic subjects. This last detail is interesting for its unusualness—most photographers don't feel the same need to know their subjects and to exchange intimacies with them to the degree Arbus did. She was fascinated by twins, triplets, and look-alikes, by true and false self-expression, by self-plurality, by masks—in short, by identity and how we get it and make it and alter it, partly by counting on others to tell us who we are, partly by being something other than what we're supposed to be. Details like these call to mind object-relations theory—in some ways a close cousin of attachment—and concepts such as splitting and projective identification, each of which I apply to Arbus's art.

I make use of script theory too—the idea that personality can be conceptualized as a set of stimulus-affect-response sequences that recur and thereby constellate the deep structure of a life. When Arbus was quite young she visited a homeless shantytown along with a governess called Mamselle. There she was briefly exposed to a way of life that her wealth and privilege had shielded her from. She calls the memory "potent." Out of this single "scene" a "script" can be extracted; the script can then be used to make sense of similar episodes and events contained within the life.

Traits, or what psychologists Robert McCrae and Paul Costa refer to as "basic endogenous tendencies," largely heritable, also have been shown to predict a variety of life outcomes. Smokers are likely to score high in neuroticism; certain facets of openness correlate with depression; extraverts tend, on average, to be happier than introverts, to possess a greater sense of well-being. There are ways, relatively minor ways, in which trait theory sheds light on some of what Arbus did and felt.

Finally, there is the material obtained from Arbus's psychotherapist, the late Helen Boigon, with whom I communicated about a number of the psychological details of Arbus's life. Boigon treated Arbus in the years immediately preceding her suicide. What she has to say raises crucially important questions and highlights neglected themes. Emerging for the first time are, among other things, a picture of Arbus's therapy, which was odd and puzzling, notable for several instances of bizarre behavior; a new version of how Arbus's life ended; an affirmation of the centrality of sex in much of what Arbus did and created; and a monumentally privileged perspective on the needs that fueled Arbus's attempts to reach out and connect with others. One thing is obvious: If the goal is to make psychological sense of a person, then speaking with her psychotherapist advances that agenda. Boigon saw and learned things no one else did. And while she is refreshingly undogmatic and non-doctrinaire, her take on Arbus's mental makeup is invaluable.

So the life selects the theory, if we let it, and the theory, once selected, begins to shuffle, shape, and reorder the life. It's an iterative process. In the end, what ideally emerges is the sense of a good fit. Life and theory work together to create a seamless-ness; they arrive, so to speak, at the same point. They converge and cohere.

I use psychology, then, to get at the deeper origins of Arbus's art. It's what Arbus lived for. It's why she's known. It may be what she died for. I'm drawn to psychobiographical methods because I expect they will get me where I want to go.

It would be foolish and more than misleading to assert that psychobiography answers every question there is about a person. It doesn't and can't. Nothing can. Lives aren't experiments, variables can't be controlled and pitted against one another post hoc. No causal model emerges. Complete objectivity, if such a thing even exists in the world, is patently unachievable. But setting

all such facts aside, it is possible to know Arbus better, to understand some of what she was up to and who she was, to investigate
reasons behind her actions, especially her need to take pictures,
and to arrive at an image—perhaps a little grainy or blurred here
and there—of the whole of her psychological life. My aim in all
this is to be as accurate as I possibly can be, and to show an
Arbus no one has ever seen before. And if a photograph is a
"secret about a secret," as Arbus famously put it, then this book
is a password. It opens up secrets. It gets you in.

Chapter 1

ESSENTIAL MYSTERIES

ONE OF PHOTOGRAPHER Diane Arbus's first pictures, she says, was of a dog. She was living at the time on Martha's Vineyard. A big mutt with Weimaraner eyes—gray eyes—arrived every day at twilight, as if to signal the oncoming night. "It was very haunting," Arbus said. "He would come and just stare at me in what seemed a very mythic way."[1] He did not bark, scratch, fetch, lick. His intent was not to play or get petted. He had little doggishness. All he did was witness. All he did, Arbus said, was look right through her. He wasn't, that is, the least bit interested in seeing what was really there. She did not think he liked her. She took a picture of him, but it wasn't very good. Or so she said.

One of Arbus's last series of photographs was of the institutionalized mentally retarded, whom she found "the strangest combination of grownup and child" she'd ever seen. These pictures were later assembled posthumously for the book *Untitled*. The light is again crepuscular. In many shots it is Halloween, so her subjects wear masks and costumes that look for the most part handmade, primitive, and thus even more eerie. They stand in pairs or threes, in groups headed for some unearthly rite, some darker oblivion. At first Arbus adored these subjects. She went back to photograph them over and over. "FINALLY what I've been searching for," she exclaimed.[2] Then she reversed her position. The pictures were no good. Her art was not doing it for her anymore, she said to a friend.[3]

Why the reversal? What weren't the photographs doing?

Shortly after this about-face, Arbus was dead. She was found on the evening of July 28, 1971, by her friend, mentor, and lover, Marvin Israel, who had been unable to reach her by phone. She was, in the words of the medical investigator, "crunched up in bath tub, on left side, wearing red shirt, blue denim shorts, no socks." She weighed one hundred pounds. The skin of her face had sloughed off "due to decomposition." Hair could also be pulled out readily. Final cause of death was listed as: "Incised wounds of wrists with external hemorrhage. Acute barbiturate poisoning."[4]

Arbus left little to chance, it seems. She wanted to die. Or did she? There had been no known prior attempt of any kind—no acts of self-harm, no grim practice runs, no suicide "rehearsal," as one often finds in such cases. By hurting herself so severely, had she really aimed to punish? But if so, whom? On the July 26 page of her appointment book she had written, ambiguously, "Last Supper." Perhaps, like Christ, she imagined a resurrection.

"Nothing about her life, her photographs, or her death was accidental or ordinary," Richard Avedon said. "They were mysterious and decisive and unimaginable, except to her. Which is the way it is with genius."

After years of seeing what no one else could or would dare to, Arbus suddenly found herself in the awkward and probably enormously disorienting position of interrogating a kind of absence: the un-self-conscious mentally retarded. All Arbus's other subjects had seen her into being. They gave her something back. They reacted to her presence. The camera made them pliable. She defined them and they returned the favor. They *were* self-conscious, and they had the effect of increasing Arbus's consciousness of her own self. The mentally retarded took far less interest. They did not meet her gaze. They exchanged no secrets. There were no intimacies. They gave off no reflection. Arbus was left alone with her single self, and it was not enough to sustain her. Her art, as she said, was not doing it for her anymore, and in crucial respects *she was her art.*

The photographer Diane Arbus is a sort of shape changer or mobile Rorschach. She was many things to many people. She came from immense wealth yet dreamed of throwing it all away, finding it loathsome and humiliating. She was more afraid than anyone else but also strangely daring, especially when it came to getting the pictures she wanted. She hated falseness and masks, yet always felt a little two-faced as she seduced her many sitters, got them to do things they later regretted. Arbus was a different person depending on what she was doing, as we all are. Even her name suggests multiplicity—some called her Diane, some "Dee-Ann." Psychologists refer to this as "domain specificity." Arbus might be tenacious and full of certitude in one endeavor—tracking down a person she wished to photograph, for instance—but unsure and insecure in another. Often there is no unifying template that provides a solution to the myriad things we do, feel, think.

Data on Arbus is relatively scarce. There is the one full-length biography, written by Patricia Bosworth and published in 1984. Bosworth interviewed a great number of people, many of whom, especially Arbus's mother, brother (poet Howard Nemerov), and sister, had plenty interesting to say; others, notably Arbus's daughter, Doon, and her ex-husband, Allan Arbus, apparently declined interviews. The portrait is slightly lopsided. The scales tilt toward Arbus's weaknesses. These no doubt existed (as they do for anyone), but they take a definite backseat to the uncanny art she made, the photographs and—an area of artistry very much neglected in Arbus's body of work—her writing, which was edgy, poetical, densely metaphoric, and startlingly accomplished.

Sylvia Plath is an interesting contrast. In her case the data is almost dauntingly abundant. Numerous full-length biographies can be consulted, as can letters, journals, hundreds of books and essays by people who became intimate with her, even a book of poems, *Birthday Letters*, by her husband, Ted Hughes, that amounts to a kind of symbolic psychobiography. The poems often aim at illuminating Plath's psychology and the motives behind her art. Though in many interesting respects very much like Plath, Arbus has been spared her degree of posthumous scrutiny and speculation. Simply put, there is quite a bit less to go on.

A hefty portion of the perplexity surrounding Arbus—who she was exactly, what she was like—comes from the artist herself. When she talked about her life, or about her work, comments tended toward the cryptic. She was gifted at creating Möbius strips of language—mini-koans. Comments like "a photograph is a secret about a secret, the more it tells you, the less you know" and "I get to keep what nobody needs" are endlessly interpretable. They leave the mystery intact. There may have been some canniness to this. Arbus, that is, may have known what she was doing. In her work she created legends; she did the same for her life. As Oscar Wilde once said, the best thing anyone can hope for is to be misunderstood. Misunderstandings only intensify the need to know more.

Then there's the Arbus estate—famously closefisted, notoriously obstreperous if not outright adversarial. It is impossible to pick up any one of the small number of books about Arbus and not find some bitter footnoted remark concerning the firm obstructionism of those tending her legacy. It must be difficult to live as the daughters of a famous person with a definite cult status who also committed suicide, for reasons that can only be guessed at. The hurt would be very deep. One might want, utterly understandably, to guard the memories one has, to fight off the invasions of the biographical body snatchers. Who, after all, owns Arbus's life? How much needs to be known, and for what purpose?

One recent event has intensified and deepened the Arbus legend: the 2003 mounting of a traveling exhibition combining some new with mostly old work, and the publication of an accompanying book, *Revelations*, the only published source containing lengthy quotes from Arbus's letters and workbooks. The book includes a partial facsimile of a childhood autobiography, contact sheets from some of Arbus's more famous shots, dreams, thoughts on psychotherapist visits, self-portraits including a nude with Arbus lying across the lap of a swinger. This is not to say, however, that much has not been withheld. Thirteen detailed and content-heavy appointment books exist covering the years 1959 to 1971, when she killed herself, alongside a total of thirty-nine notebooks spanning the same years. *Revelations* samples cautiously from this treasure trove, yet how much has been left out, and for what reason, is impossible to determine. Arbus, for her part, was not always and inevitably coy. For instance, in 1970 she readily responded to a series of questions from a Georgia State University student she had never met, a woman named Gail Lineback who expressed interest in Arbus's work. The estate, however, has been far more chary, to a degree Arbus herself might have found excessive.

It is hard deciding what to make of this cache of new primary material anyway. What revelations did *Revelations* contain? Not a great number. The total effect is to lend substance to what had been guessed at already. Funnily enough, although the book was obviously intended as a corrective to Bosworth's melancholic unsubtleties, it actually winds up confirming her vision. As the always trenchant Janet Malcolm observed in her review, "Arbus comes out looking just as brooding and morbid and sexually perverse and absurd."[5] But she's no less a puzzle, and the reasons for her perversity, her absurdity, remain intriguingly obscure.

The core mystery, of course, is Arbus's immediate and abiding interest in subjects she called "freaks." These were people who had passed some supreme test in life, who had stood up and answered a difficult question, solved a potentially soul-shattering riddle. The latter lent them, in Arbus's eyes, a certain glamour; they were, in her estimation, "anonymously famous." We all possess this anxiety, Arbus once explained, about whether or not we can be strong enough, secure enough, when the time comes, to face off against an adversary, to conquer fear, to take on vexing moral questions. To her, freaks had proved their mettle. They had demonstrated their resolve. They passed the test. So partly for this very reason—along with numberless others, no doubt—they became her foremost occupation. She tracked them down with ferocity. She joked about being Jewish and rich and from a good family and running away from it all giddily. In a Guggenheim application of 1962 she describes her subjects: sideshows, secret photos of steam bathers, female impersonators. Locations include Times Square, Central Park, Automats, Grand Central Station, the Roller Derby, rodeos, circuses, Harlem dance halls, wax museums, pool houses, and, above all, a place that would bewitch her mightily, Hubert's Dime Museum and Flea Circus.

In October 1959 Arbus started work for *Esquire* magazine on an issue devoted to New York. This gave way to an independent photographic essay, a project on the city ranging from "the posh to the sordid."[6] She visits Mother Cabrini, a disinterred saint. She checks out the Mr. Universe Health Parlor. She loiters in meat markets waiting for the heads. She meets Walter Gregory, "the Madman from Massachusetts," a legendary Bowery character. The mad man waved his finger in her face saying "who was I?"[7] He had just one eye, and his nose was folded over. "I don't press the shutter," she tells Marvin Israel. "The image does. And it's like being gently clobbered."[8] Around the same time she wonders, "I think it does, a little, hurt to be photographed."[9]

In July 1960, Arbus's "The Vertical Journey: Six Movements of a Moment Within the Heart of the City" appeared in *Esquire*, along with captions of Arbus's devising. The spread signaled her arrival. Already she was interested in blurring boundaries between the fantastical and the mundane. The closer one looks, the odder one's objects of perception get. Flaws, always a particular fascination, have their way of rising to the surface. Hezekiah Trambles, "the Jungle Creep," comes off as far more affrighted than creepy. His position suggests he's under attack. Mrs. Dagmar Patino, photographed at the Grand Opera Ball benefiting Boystown of Italy, is no less degraded. The photo is grainy. Her black eyes float pellucidly beneath a jewel of some sort holding her hair in place on top of her head. Her arms cross stolidly, a look of faint disapproval on her face. The scene is one big hallucinatory swirl. Nothing achieves clarity. We also meet Andrew Ratoucheff, a dwarf actor known for his imitations of Marilyn Monroe and Maurice Chevalier; a shirtless, tattooed Walter Gregory, his right eye sealed shut, lips oddly asymmetrical; the meditative Flora Knapp Dickinson, Honorary Regent of the Washington Heights Chapter of the Daughters of the American Revolution. Then there is "person unknown" from the city morgue, tag affixed to his right big toe. The fact is, these are all persons unknown. Or if we think we know them, we know less than we think. What is freakier, anomalousness or normality?

All these human oddities Arbus compared to characters in a spooky fairy tale for grown-ups. Rumpelstiltskin-like, they stopped you in your tracks. If Arbus's clicked image constitutes an answer, it applies equally to her subjects and to herself. "There are always two things that happen," she said. "One is recognition and the other is that it's totally peculiar. But *there's some sense in which I always identify with them.*"[10] The pictures are Arbus's internal world externalized. The secrets she exposed were hers—theirs too, but hers.

The most significant early work on freaks appeared in *Harper's Bazaar* in November 1961 under the title "The Full Circle." Here we discover not only photographs but a great deal of written text composed by Arbus herself. In July 1961, Arbus writes to her sixteen year-old daughter Doon, "I spent the weekend of the fourth holed up writing about twelve hours a day on the rest of the Odd People."[11] *Esquire* passed on the piece, asking Arbus to destroy or return her letter of accreditation—a credentials statement regularly provided to members of the media who are present at events. Concerns were raised about publishing pictures of people for the sole purpose of showing them as eccentrics. *Harper's Bazaar*, then guided by the twin visions of Marvin Israel and Richard Avedon, both of whom apparently wished to push the magazine into uncharted territory, saw its way around such legal landmines. Arbus was both relieved and troubled. "I'm glad to stop thinking about it," she confessed, "because praise is very unsettling."[12] This reaction proved to be a common one: "I'm not as good a photographer as people think except sometimes and in my head."[13] Her work mattered most to her; she could not stop working. Yet success unnerved her.

Whatever the case, the publication marked Arbus as an artist of distinction and promise. Her subjects she calls metaphors. She sought out the ideal eccentric, the man who ties himself in knots. She shot the Backwards Man who sees where he was. Such people are beckoned, not driven. It is their fate to be who they are: heroes of a real dream, constantly tested and tried.

As Arbus told *Newsweek* in 1967, "It's irrational to be born in a certain place and time and of a certain sex. It's irrational how much you can change circumstance and how much you can't. The whole idea of me being born rich and Jewish is part of that irrationality. But if you're born one thing, you can dare— venture—to be ten thousand other things." Arbus pursued a supplemental life, an abundance of selves instead of the one she'd been stuck with. The life she had been thrown into struck her as irrational in the sense that it seemed so much at odds with what she felt inside. It was not something she could live with.

Freaks, to Arbus at least, are notable for their absolute certitude. These people are miraculously undaunted in Arbus's idealizing eyes. Jack Dracula, the marked man, embellished with 306 tattoos, lies on his side in a field of grass. His tattoo mask comes at a price, like any mask, for the dye covering his body turns poisonous on prolonged exposure to the sun. He can outstare any stranger, we learn. He looks large, proud, aloof. Friends and enemies alike respect him "but there is no one he cannot do without."[14] Arbus calls him a privileged exile. It's a posture they obviously share. As Arbus herself observed, "overprivileged children of tycoons are almost toomuchblessed as freaks."[15]

William Mack, another early subject, is an awesome figure even at age seventy-two. He must be fearsomely strong, Arbus notes, carrying as he does great sacks of bottles on his shoulders. Sometimes people give him money, though they seldom dare to. Life makes no sense, he intones. He calls it a pack of lies, it means nothing. Another powerful, brave man is Prince Robert de Rohan Courtenay, his Serene Highness, surnamed the Magnificent. He lives in a bejeweled, encrusted, embellished, bedizened six-by-nine-foot room called the Jade Tower, under a ceiling of orchids and painted butterflies. Arbus singles out this passage from his writings: "The facets of a man's life so vary, in a seeming and rapid inconsistency, that he appears to live his life as a succession of characters . . . The personal history of anyone is merely a legend, imperfectly understood." Max Maxwell Landar, or Uncle Sam, shot in front of a group of blurry children (laundry drying on a makeshift line above their heads) who look to be following Maxwell in the direction of some alternate America, makes a similar point about self's multiplicity: "I am what I call a Personality . . . I could be other people . . . I am a Phenomenon."

These are the "Odd People" whom Arbus always found irrepressible. Together they constituted a mutual support system, all trying to be somehow more than they were, all—like Arbus—in search of ten thousand other possible lives. The one self they had was not enough. Their portraits were "the products of a kind of mutual seduction which Arbus instigated by being herself seduced," according to daughter Doon in the October 1972 issue of *Ms.* magazine. She began her artistic life as a "huntress, and it seemed that the more she discovered, the more she became her own prey. She was like someone pursued." The pictures weren't so much about what she drew from people but what people drew from her. "Even if she was only with them for a few hours, she exchanged secrets."

This need to expose hidden territories carried with it certain paradoxes that would give Arbus trouble. Her sitters were both masked and embodied, somehow more real *because* of their costumes—authentically phony. But they are, at the same time, divided. They are who they are, but they are other people besides. Each life is a congress of characters, personality a multiplicity. I could be other people, Maxwell declared pompously. Arbus would go on to shoot hundreds of pictures of twins and triplets, couples, siblings, look-alikes. In a series of portraits taken of Arbus by Saul Leiter in November 1970, the wall in front of which she sits is plastered with dualities, side-by-side faces difficult to tell apart. These people were eccentrics too. In fact, she refers to a twin convention as the perfect eccentric event. Even her last major series of pictures focusing on the mentally retarded returned to the topic of masks and masklessness. These subjects grabbed her partly because of their total absence of self-consciousness, their guilelessness, and, in a sense, emptiness. They don't seem to possess a self, not at least in the sense of something one actively constructs. They are masked *and* maskless, nothing and something at the very same time.

The publication of "The Full Circle" was not, per usual for Arbus, an altogether happy event. She tells her brother in December 1961, "I been gloomy. Publication . . . felt a little like an obituary . . ." She can't seem to figure out why she feels no sense of triumph, no sense of achievement or accomplishment. All there is is sadness, directionlessness. Her visions of the world everyone else seems to find obscene. Not quite one year later she calls herself a "tightrope walker who might fall if somebody screamed."[17]

Sex is a mystery in Arbus's life too, but it's left mostly marginalized—and all the more mysterious—in biographical writings. A stunning absence, given the clear sexual content of much of her work. Even when sex isn't front and center, it insidiously works its way into shots, a whispering directorial voice. Patricia Bosworth refers to acts of erotic adventurousness but fails to ask what the sexual behavior *meant* for Arbus or what *function* it may have served, nor does she explore its presence in the art, an omission I try to remedy here. But the work speaks for itself. Couples of all types enthralled her, as did nudists, swingers, transvestites. In May 1968 she speaks of her work going along obsessively, and of wanting to shoot "empurpled whores."[18] Photography, she confesses, "is a . . . private sin of mine."[19]

April 1969 finds her in London on assignment; in her imagination the town must conceal hordes of nasty secrets. But they prove next to impossible to find. The world and the people in it obstinately refuse to live out her fantasies of darkness and misery. "Where have they hidden it," she wonders?[20]

All this is in keeping with Arbus's primary agenda: seeing what others have not, finding what has been covered over. Life was a kind of Potemkin village. Her business was to expose the hoax. Sex is *the* most brilliant unknown territory, in some ways the final, inevitable frontier, Arbus's manifest destiny. An example of this interest (among many) is the 1970 photo called "Dominatrix with a Kneeling Client." The man looks middle-aged. He wears black socks up to his knees and a black hood on his head. The woman stands above him in a bustier and latex boots, black mesh nylons barely concealing an imperfect triangle of heavy black pubic hair. *Revelations* also includes a contact sheet, number 4457, of a couple sitting on a couch. In most shots she is naked; he has his shirt off. They kiss and cuddle. It all seems perfectly harmless, playful. Yet a single image stands out, taken, it would seem, by the woman or someone else on hand. This time it is Arbus who is naked. She lies across the man's lap as he smiles broadly, his hand on Arbus's right thigh. Arbus grasps his knee, her expression a little uncertain, more bland than aroused.

In 1968 Arbus shot the filming of a pornographic movie. It's an endlessly comic affair. The men are enormously self-conscious and "turtlenecked." Their eyes, in a kind of crazed nystagmus, roll over Arbus's body like "balls on a pinball machine."[21]

Arbus mentions a 1969 contact she made with erotologists Phyllis and Eberhard Kronhausen, editors of collections of erotic art and promoters of sex causes. Apparently they had private patients whom they analyzed by living in their homes. Arbus calls the couple self-appointed apostles of sex. Though she records their eagerness to be photographed by her, in the end the idea leaves her feeling squeamish: "It gives me a funny eerie sense of mutual exploitation."[22] Later I explore in detail how this particular session came to its very revealing conclusion. Arbus, it seems, found herself suddenly aroused. She confessed wanting to have sex with the couple, and because of this, she could not shoot. It was to be one of the very few occasions when the camera failed her.

The pursuit of this taboo domain was not, then, merely intellectual or limited to its assembled imagery. Arbus also tested her own limits. In her therapy with Dr. Helen Boigon, she spoke of picking up "queer-looking" (i.e., odd-appearing) men on the street and having sex with them.[23] She wasn't always successful. What she was searching for, according to Boigon, was *experience*. "That's all she could name it."

The role played by sexual desire in Arbus's art, and the effect of her sexual life on her personality, call for some kind of elucidation. If the doing of art always siphons a quota of its energy from sexuality, then by way of reverse causality creativity makes of the artist a sexualized being. Certain writers, poet Philip Larkin for instance, have spoken at length about this very nexus. The vision required of the artist, Larkin figures, has "got something to do with sex. I don't know what, and I don't particularly want to know. It's not surprising because obviously two creative voices would be in alliance. But the vision has a sexual quality lacking in other emotions such as pity . . . Ovid, for instance, could never write unless he was in love. Many other poets have been and are the same. I should think poetry and sex are very closely connected." It's important to keep in mind the fact that Arbus was always working at the very limit of her zone of comfort. Her art was one way of dealing intensely and publicly with the forbidden. It was, as she said, a sin that she confessed to the world. There was always something perverse about it. It was a means to experiences denied or off-limits to the less adventurous. Seeing as she made little distinction between her life and her art, it makes perfect sense that the one would transform and make demands on the other. Boundaries were breached. She was, with her camera, a participant observer, but she also put her camera down and became pure participant. This was, for her, a deeper mode of knowing her subject.

One of the most encompassing mysteries of all about Arbus concerns how she managed to convince people to let her take their picture in the first place. The images themselves can be hard to figure; but so can the question of how she got them. What she liked best was to go "where I've never been," she says—such as the homes of total strangers.[24] She compares the process to a blind date. There's a queasiness to it, no means of control. She finds it annoying the way she comes off. "I'm kind of two-faced . . . I'm . . . too nice. Everything is Oooo."[25]

Many of Arbus's sessions ended up in bedrooms. People she only slightly or just accidentally knew allowed her access to their most intimate, private geographies. They were sometimes fully nude, their lovers lying beside them. Sometimes they had just awakened, in states of relative disarray. Lonely naked men might be clasping bathetically their paid consorts, with little left to the imagination. Cross-dressers and prostitutes sat in the midst of the residue of their disordered lives, ashtrays, beer cans, crumpled papers and the like strewn across the floor and the bed. Arbus obviously realized something important very early on: Just like her, people wanted to be seen. The camera provided a kind of harsh yet undeniable attention people believed they deserved. It was a scrutiny to which they felt entitled. They wanted someone to make legends out of them, and Arbus obliged. No doubt they sensed her sympathy. She must have made it clear that she understood, in precise terms, their unique predicament, the challenge they faced. She must also have had an enormous talent for eliciting trust—it would be okay, these people may have reasoned, to show this woman things I've never shown anyone else, and to let her keep a part of me, and then perhaps to show this part to the world in general.

The sharing of secrets played a vital role. Secrets were what Arbus coveted. She kept them, and bore down on them in others. The theme of the secret—what it meant to Arbus and how it featured in her life and art—is another core mystery. A feature common to every Arbus shoot was confession. She bared select secrets. She provided that context. The picture was to be all about honesty, authenticity, messy repressed reality. Her subjects bought the assumption and either offered up what she wanted them to or else found themselves, a little or a lot

AN EMERGENCY IN SLOW MOTION

against their will, getting "Arbused." In the end, after all, it was always Arbus who decided which secret was most real. The miracle is that her sitters felt understood enough by her to accept that devil's bargain.

Many have marveled at the fearlessness of this small woman risking life and limb in dark, dangerous places in order to get the kinds of photos she assiduously collected, but it was precisely her vulnerability that made the art possible. It was her smallness, her femaleness, and more than anything else her terrible obsessive earnestness that made her so seductive and so disarming. She was a sympathy genius. And if part of that genius was phony, part of it was also agonizingly sincere. She became the mirror that she never had. She was the secrets holder—she illuminated the things never seen before, suppressed needs and identities.

Last is the fact of Arbus's suicide, an inevitable terminus, the product of converging reasons and needs—some more pressing than others. The art had temporarily stopped exciting and inspiring her; she was depressed. Both daughters were away (Amy at summer school in Massachusetts; Doon in Paris). Arbus was at odds with her lover Marvin Israel (who was vacationing with his wife, Maggie, on Fire Island); ex-husband Allan was in Santa Fe filming a movie (*Greaser's Palace*). Her sitters at the time, the mentally retarded, gave her nothing back, they did not relate, they did not share intimacies. As Arbus herself said to friends, her art was not "doing it for [her] anymore."[26] There were also money troubles. She was taking jobs that she found dispiriting. Boigon calls Arbus "schizoid," a term suggesting a personality disorder marked by oddness, eccentricity, and magical thinking.

Lisette Model, her mentor, found her work full of "neurosis" and "schizophrenia."[27] But whether Arbus was in some sense mentally ill when she took her life is another possibility to consider, not that it amounts to any kind of explanation. Disease labels are just that—labels. Merely names for sets of behaviors, they can't, by definition, render those behaviors psychologically understandable.

It is always a temptation, in the life of an artist who suicides, to scan the art for clues, omens. But such correlations can be purely illusory. Contiguity does not equal causality. In what follows, I do not argue that the pictures of the mentally retarded had something essential to do with Arbus's death, but they did present a dilemma for her. They increased her awareness of conflicts centering on self, conflicts that had always been present but not consciously so. One point deserves some mention in passing. Art is not intrinsically therapeutic. It doesn't always allow us to rise above. Instead, it can be an immersion in products of self-expression that mirror our troubles back at us so that we see them metaphorically, but still glaringly. Then it's a matter of what we do with this information, what we make of it. We can turn away again, re-repress what we've inadvertently discovered, or try some means of assimilation. My guess is that Arbus was working to assimilate the meaning that the photos of the retarded revealed to her in the months and weeks before she died. Her death cut the connection-making process short. The psychological business was left unfinished.

A question about Arbus's suicide is whether or not she wanted to die. That she both slit her wrists and took what appears to be an overdose seems to rule out any possibility of doubt but, on the other hand, things are never quite that simple. Though it may sound paradoxical and even illogical, plenty of people intend *and* don't intend to die when they make an attempt on their own life. They are ambivalent. They also often have no way of knowing if the act will succeed, and some frankly don't care, because either way their situation will be radically altered. Was Arbus in emotional pain at the time of her death? Yes. Did she want the pain to end? Yes. Did she want her *life* to end? That question takes the discussion to a different level. One can also ask about Arbus: Did she want her art to end? Here I'm certain the answer is no.

The fact of suicide always seems to require the articulation of a dark motive. It waves the reading of a life down morbid avenues. My goal, however, in investigating Arbus's death is to understand the behavior's *function*. In other words (and this can't sound anything but a little preposterous on its face), what was she hoping to get out of it, regardless of its success or failure?

In 1959 Arbus recorded a dream in her first notebook, one she repeats in May 1971 for an *Artforum* spread titled, simply, "Five Photographs by Diane Arbus." Like many dreams, this one tells of an undeniable psychological reality.

She finds herself on an ocean liner resembling "Ship Beautiful," the one she wrote about in a childhood autobiography. It's decorated ornately, flamboyantly. All at once she notices smoke and registers the fact that the ship's on fire. It seems as if they must be sinking, but no one appears to care. The party obliviously continues. Though all hope fades, Arbus is euphoric. "I could photograph anything I wanted to."

In the original iteration, from 1959, she is hurried, and she wants to photograph "most awfully." The setting is not an ocean liner, but a hotel. Her grandmother is around. She has no clue how to proceed, how to behave. She continues: "It's like the sinking Titanic . . . My whole life is there . . . I am strangely alone although people are all around. They keep disappearing . . . It's like an emergency in slow motion."[28]

This dream is yet another mystery. Her life's on fire, her life is sinking, but everyone is gay and dancing and singing. If she does not know exactly what she's looking for, one thing is certain: She has to photograph. She may be alone among people, people may be disappearing, there may be no hope, but she's terribly elated. Her art will put out the fire. Her art will save her.

Chapter 2

THE SECRET

M IXED IN WITH shots of livid Puerto Rican women, men who swallow razor blades, and dominatrixes with sallow, bespectacled, tax-accountant clients are the babies Arbus now and then aimed herself at. Her best-known baby subject was Anderson Cooper, of CNN's *AC 360*. Wet-lipped and puffy-cheeked, wrapped in soft white cotton, Cooper—shot in 1968—looks positively beatific, as if he'd just relinquished the nipple, orgasmically sated. No harm will visit him, that's for sure. Behind his closed eyes he does not dream of darkness. Other Arbus babies aren't so lucky. Most of these shots came from diaper derbies, where babies get placed on their knees in a tent, usually in groups of three, and crawl desultorily toward some arbitrary finish line, or else compete in contests like "most voluminous drool." These infants, far more abundant in Arbus's portfolio, never look happy, or proud, or victorious, or even sedate. They cry. They fume. Their sweat-faced mothers jam them into the camera lens. It's a dark, crazy world from which the babies better not expect any comfort or encouraging attention. It is as if they've gotten hip to their own predicament; they know they're defense-less against emotional injury. There are problems and bigger problems and that's about it. They can cry all they want, but A.E. Housman was right: It rains into the sea, and still the sea is salt.

It's funny, one shot contrasts the human infants with some-thing altogether different but similar: a woman with her baby monkey, taken in 1971, the year of Arbus's death. The woman's proud, with a half smile. The monkey's in her lap on a couch, with baby outfit and baby bonnet. It's a gruesome scene, maca-bre in the extreme, but somehow more reassuring than the real babies and their real mothers. The monkey is loved, fiercely. The real babies don't appear to be.

Arbus's life was not like the monkey's.

What's essential to investigate is the prehistory of Diane Arbus's appetite for looking, with which, a little miraculously in light of the freakish pictures she took, the viewer of the photographs colludes. Arbus makes us want to see the same things she did. It's as if she found the peephole and we looked through it, over and over. Franz Kafka said, "One photographs things in order to get them out of one's mind." The pictures are a kind of clos-ing of one's eyes. What was Arbus getting *out*?

Her life's outline isn't terribly unfamiliar. She passed from bright light, from a world of wealth in which she felt like a privileged exile, into darkness, the worlds of her subjects. In fact, she did more: She lit up the darkness and in so doing gave the darkness eyes to see. She went down to a kind of hell, a region of the hidden, to extract and bring back up for inspec-tion a collection of images that, though in some ways right in front of us, we had nevertheless always refused to perceive. She looked hard at these things and made sure they looked back. There was a time when she thought, probably only for a moment, that she might like to be a psychiatrist; her art is a sort of uncovering, like all great art, both for her and her audience. It is the record of our disavowals. Though we had always passed these pictures by, when they reemerge we *recognize* them. They are the impurities we threw aside. They are the secrets we never got to the bottom of. And if Arbus was about anything, she was about secrets. Secrets were her subject. She found them and she shared them, simultaneously. Her pictures confessed.

Her early years, along with what she said about them in hindsight, must signal something as to why she felt such a powerful need to uncover what she called her sense of "contagion" out there. Early years don't ever tell us everything we need to know about a person, of course, but they can't be elbowed aside, either, in some sort of anti-Freudian jettisoning. They put dynamics in motion. They lead to relational strategies, trademark ways of responding to distress especially. Arbus's brother, the poet Howard Nemerov, in his book *Journal of the Fictive Life*, explains how "It is not my childhood that I seek, but the childhood of my art. As much to say, Mommy, where do images come from?"[1] The same could be asked of Arbus, who collected "naughty" images. Where did *her* images come from? She was inclined to note that she always suffered as a child from a feeling of immunity and exemption. Like the historical Buddha, there were encounters she was to be shielded from. She sought a wound she actually already had. Or else she sought to make the wound *public*.

Diane Arbus was born Diane Nemerov on March 14, 1923, the middle child of Gertrude and David Nemerov. Her brother,

Howard, was three at the time; a younger sister, Renee, arrived five years later, in 1928. Solid data on Arbus's early years is scarce. What others have said about her life as a child will be examined below—her brother's recollections, her mother's, and those of Renee, who calls her own childhood "almost like imprisonment."[2] But suicide has a way of darkening all remembrances; a sort of gloomy, clue-seeking reconstruction is difficult to avoid.

In this case, however, there are two enormously interesting childhood autobiographies, both written as class assignments, one when Arbus was ten (it's dated September 29, 1934), the other when she was fourteen. The first is sweet and breezy, cheerful, the second far more dark, dense, emotionally fraught—it sets an emotional atmosphere, a tone, that never left her. It documents personality patterns, fears and needs that carried over into adult life.[3]

The first essay is ten wide-spaced pages long, titled "My Autobiography." There's a hand-drawn picture on the cover in which the "Babyhood" Diane wears a one-piece dress. Her hair lightly covers her head, mostly bald. She seems to hold something in her right hand, or else it's just smudged; her left arm is muscular, like a comic book superhero's. There is also a table of contents broken down into nine sections, including (among others) Family, Birth, Memories, Things I Don't Like, and Things I Like.

In strikingly lovely handwriting, she begins by confessing a basic uncertainty. She can't be sure if her memories match reality. It is going to be necessary, she explains, to inject some fantasy into the biographical record. She invites readers to suspend doubt, to enter a space of shared imagination.

Her mother, Gertrude, she can't conjure. The picture is blurry, indistinct. She is busy, most likely, anticipating Diane's arrival, planning her name. Her father, the wealthy furrier David Nemerov, she sees more clearly. He's got a mustache, he's smoking, he's tall. He flips back and forth in his mind between two exciting possibilities—girl or boy? He betrays no preference. He simply wonders, more or less happily.

Diane's brother Howard Nemerov comes first in the tale, as he did in life. She senses he's hoping for a sister, even if, after she arrives, all they seem to do is fight. Then, skipping ahead five years Renee emerges, a sister whom Diane secretly wanted to name Mary or Greta after a pair of girls she knew from school. Her own birth she precisely records: March 14, 1923, at one thirty in the morning. In her imagination she's large, incongruously blonde and blue-eyed, a pear-shaped, red-cheeked beauty.

A few slight memories stand out, but nothing terribly spectacular or startling. In his own autobiography, written many years later, Howard recalls Diane accidentally cutting herself with a China doll; Diane recounts the same incident. Its saliency for both of them implies a deeper meaning, but one never fleshed-out. There are sweet moments with the younger Renee. She and Diane sequester themselves in a bedroom, reading and sharing funny stories. Several paragraphs focus on the family trip to France on the RMS *Aquitania*, a Cunard ocean liner launched in 1913 and nicknamed "Ship Beautiful." One morning Diane secretly orders bananas and cold cereal, against her governess's wishes. There is a run-in with a silly goat, of which Diane was terrified. He's tied up, he stands implacably, with a sort of native stoicism, a bit like the myth-encrusted dog that would later become one of Arbus's first photographs.

School is mostly fun but Diane often feels nervous and different. Graduation leaves her trembling; she worries about making a mistake during the silent, oppressive ceremony. As a gift she receives a large new bicycle, a fine reward despite her nervousness. About math she is ambivalent. Sometimes she wishes it might disappear from the face of the earth. Of all animals bats scare her most. In pictures they look impossibly fearsome.

Wishing to end on a positive note, she recalls her love of chocolate ice cream.

Apart from trace amounts of normal shyness and fear, Diane comes through as upbeat, untroubled, optimistic. The mood is sunny. But at fourteen the sun goes into eclipse. A very different, far darker world emerges, full of hate, distrust, secrets, doom, and terrible sadness. It's a jarring contrast. We seem to meet a different person.

Here again, in dense, tiny, handwritten prose, Arbus sees herself as roly-poly—blonde, red-cheeked—but the world is on fire, she's always hot, always inconsolable. What she wants to do, more than anything else, is sleep. The gauze of sleep is constant; she means it not in any symbolic sense, but physically. Sleep is where tumult dissipates. She strongly resists being awakened. If people try rousing her, she's angry, she yells and detests them. These unsettled feelings are now and then alleviated by Diane's French governess, Mamselle, who took care of her for the first seven years of her life, but even Mamselle has a troubled, stern, unreadable face. There is something she is not saying, something she will never tell anyone. Secrets in fact make for the essay's main theme; it's hard not to wonder whether Mamselle's sad secret is truly hers or Diane's projected. But no matter. Diane adores her. She can't live without her. She does all she can to make her stay, always. Occasional vacations elicit, from Diane, hot tears and neediness. Love is always just tenuously around; if it leaves, as Mamselle did occasionally, there is no guarantee of return.

Diane decides she needs a motto, a solid, immortal life anchor that will magically make everything right. She casts about for an ideal choice, at last settling on "In God we trust." She is puffed up with pride; she swears she'll never waver. God won't disappoint. But even with Him (or Her) up there somewhere, a reassuring sentry, steady and available, trust remains in perilously short supply. Arbus can't seem to find it in mortals. Betrayal crouches around every corner. And there's a reason: a fear that never left Diane, a need to which she was unendingly tethered. *She held secrets*, some modest, some large. They vibrated restively. What they are, exactly, she never says. They must be sad, like Mamselle's. There do not seem to be any other kind. Yet to a long line of girls, confidants Arbus sought out and cultivated, she tremblingly confides, over and over. Secrets leak out in cooking class, at camp, by the waterside. There is this constant need to release something hidden, an inner burden; it's an impulse also at the root of Arbus's later photography, her adult art, which she called a private sin. But the girls prove to be poor containers. The secrets don't stay that way. They get tossed back in Arbus's face humiliatingly. The exchanges leave her sick, disgusted, red-faced.

An identical script repeats itself—a need to trust, expose, confide, the risk of sharing followed by rejection. One girl after another enacts her role. Arbus enjoys the intense closeness she manages to manufacture, but it becomes too much. The girls wear one another out. There is a fakeness, a straining. Arbus decides she can't like the girls as much as she needs to. In the end, no burden is ever lifted. The load isn't lightened. Diane reaches the conclusion that scores of people held her secrets, that she wanted to love them but couldn't, that they failed to respect the intimacies she shared. She is left with a sense of dullness. She's angry at herself, disgusted by her weird confession compulsion. Maybe, she concludes, it is best to leave things mysterious, obscure. Being understood is being known a little too well. Arbus isn't sure she likes it.

Drama and intrigue in fourteen-year-old girls is anything but unexpected. Feelings get hurt constantly, love and hate vacillate daily, triangles abound (girls B and C both want girl A to like them best, and so on), tears fall. But several things make what Arbus describes in her autobiography unaverage. The general sense of distrust is one. No one can be counted on. An intense need for closeness is another. And in Arbus this need alternates with feelings of hatred toward those she also admires. She wants intimacy and understanding but when she gets it, it bugs her. Then there's the glaringly important feature of secrets— needing to find someone to tell hers to, someone who will respect them. But the confessions end in betrayal. Her sins are broadcast.

What worked to magnify this sense of sin was a nasty and punitive conscience. She couldn't control it, she says, she couldn't disobey it. Often it would shower, from inside, ghastly curses that scared her to death. She was ashamed of herself, but she was also ashamed of anything she was connected with: her family (who did things the wrong way), her school (which taught her erroneous facts), and her father's business (badly, even criminally, run). One way Arbus dealt with this internal persecutor, a superego on steroids, was by projecting it onto others or even the world at large. She says she saw evil in every face. She feared kidnappers, so when anyone did come up to her—men in particular—she would wave at a person blocks away, pretending to know him or her, then run.

Over and over she tells little stories of minor, trivial wrongs, such as lying to an art teacher about cleaning a brush. She's anguished and self-lacerating, but the reaction is incommensurate to the actual deed, the guilt misplaced. There's the sense—unavoidable, really—that these minor confessions screen something major. She confesses them when what she really wants to confess are the secrets: It's the secrets to whom the guilt belongs and from which the guilt derives. In the dense, five-page autobiography fragment available, Arbus never comes clean about these secrets, though in the full, unavailable document she may. It's a core component of the grown-up art too, which she called a secret about a secret. The more it tells you, the less you know. The impulse to both say and not say, to be understood and unknown, never left her.

Around age twelve, Arbus says, everyone determined she was an artist. She was given lessons and a big box of oils. She painted and drew for about four years. But she was, as usual, conflicted. On one hand, she used to pray and wish often to be "a great sad artist," but at the same time she doubted her ability, believed she didn't know what she was doing. It was all show, all pretense, the congratulations insincere. Her adult reaction to success was no different; it made her feel besieged and paranoid.

Firsts of different kinds can be revealing, like Arbus's first stab at making art. She also talks about what she calls her first "sin": losing cards of multiplication problems while pretending she had them all along. And she remembers her first dream (or vision, or memory). It's a picture of the corner of her room, seen from bed. The walls and ceiling meet in a vague light and a "ball of black wool" sits on air in the corner "with one end a little un-twisted."

One of Arbus's first memories concerns a similar sort of blackness—what one can't see, but for different reasons. In a 1968 radio interview with Studs Terkel, she refers once more to an early life filled with governesses—the one she loved (Mamselle) and a succession of others she didn't. "I remember going with this governess that I loved—*liked*—to the park [Central Park in New York City], to the site of the reservoir which had been drained; it was just a cavity and there was this shantytown there. For years I couldn't get anyone to remember this, but finally someone at the Museum of the City of New York said yes, there was this shantytown. This image wasn't concrete, but for me it was a potent memory. Seeing the other side of the tracks holding the hand of one's governess. For years I felt exempt. I grew up exempt and immune from circumstance. The idea that I couldn't wander down . . . and that there is such a gulf. I keep learning this over and over again . . . My brother and I never went far afield . . . the outside world was so far. Not evil, but the doors were simply shut. You never expected to encounter it. For so long I lived as if there was contagion. I guess you would call it innocence, but I wouldn't call it pretty at all . . ."[4]

As one of the few readily available scraps an adult Arbus ever offered about her childhood, the shantytown scene has special salience. It is hard to resist. And in fact it points to several themes. First, there is the scene's apparent prototype quality: It is a blueprint for the core parameters of her life history. Even as a small child, Arbus was pulled down to darkness, to a world she had been denied; the shantytown is a little like the image of the black ball of wool sitting on air—fascinating, vaguely lighted. She wanted badly to "go down," to be, in a word, an adventurer—yet she could not do so. She was refused this license, and the refusal pained her. Or the *idea* of it did, looking back as an adult. The reservoir cavity, a literal hole in the ground, is a sort of visual unconscious, containing all those things one was expected to leave alone, to repress ("the doors were simply shut"). So as an adult, Arbus remedied the privation. She made it her mission to see what she was not supposed to—secrets— and she took her camera with her, as talisman, in the process helping others find the same darkness—*forcing* others to find it. As if to say: This is what was denied me, and it was denied you too. The pictures were the proof of the night journey she had taken.[5] Taking them was a way of doing what she had always wanted to do but couldn't. In this respect, the art itself was a form of acting out; by doing it she was getting away with something. It suggested revolt, perhaps mainly against her mother, Gertrude, whom Renee calls "very conventional, and very kind of anti anything strange."[6] If Arbus's work was anything, it was *strange*. The strangeness made it dirty.

Second, there is the remark concerning exemption and immunity, the feeling of being forced to participate in a kind of lie her privilege made necessary. Fake innocence was not innocence. There was something sordid about it. In her adolescent diary Arbus records how she detested fickle people. She later avidly sought the real, the unmasked (as did quite a few other photographers). The shantytown memory symbolizes this desire. There is something notably counterphobic about it. If contagion is what you fear, the message seems to be, then go into the fear, inoculate yourself. In her autobiography, Arbus recalls afternoons of game playing and rock climbing. She is always the brave one, the girl who takes risks when everyone else demurs, chickens-out. Though she is secretly terrified—maybe more than anyone else, in fact—she earns a daredevil reputation. Fear, it seems, had to be faced and defeated. It's an attitude persisting through-out Arbus's life; it was also characteristic of her first and most important mentor, the photographer Lisette Model, who battled her own anxieties to get the pictures she wanted. Arbus practiced a private version of what clinical psychologists call exposure therapy: counterphobically doing exactly those things that you dread most and thereby moving past the hang-up.

David Nemerov, Arbus's father, was merchandising director at Russek's, one of the city's leading furriers. The store was founded in the 1880s by his father-in-law, Frank Russek, along with two brothers. Russek's expanded in 1924; it was reformed as a department store specializing in women's fashions. David Nem-erov was a strong proponent of this shift. In time he became vice president and fashion director; the family occasionally traveled to Europe, attending couture unveilings and assessing the latest fashion trends. Wealth was something Arbus found revolting. By far the most conspicuous facts of her early life—entitlement, luxury, immunity, exemption—all these repulsed her. Paradoxi-cally, it was painful not to hurt, not to have to wait in bread-lines like everyone else. She felt somehow half-alive, her sensations muted. She pictures herself a princess in some humiliating, "loathsome movie," at once "privileged and doomed."[7] In her father's store, as she walked the aisles beside her mother on lazy afternoons, mannequins sneered, live people bowed resentfully. "It all seemed to belong to me and I was ashamed."[8]

All these memories start to add up, a little ominously. If one pauses for a moment to take the temperature of Arbus's emotional world—always an important thing to get a solid handle on in any life study—these are the feelings emerging: crankiness, screaming, yelling, anger, shame, guilt, distrust, fear of abandonment, agony, doom, humiliation. The use of the word *hate* is common. There is the sense of a basic thwartedness, of needs not being met. Also, it's hard not to notice an absence of love, or real care and sympathy; Renee, too, speaks of being "very little loved." When Arbus does find love—with Mamselle—or closeness—with newfound friends at camp—she fears losing it, and the prospect of loss feels like a death. Her attachments, in psychological terms, are insecure, the interior a frightening place to be. And experimental research on attachment insecurity—a sense, in the young child and later in the adult, that primary caregivers will not reliably provide love and support in times of distress—does in fact reveal that anxiously attached individuals "have ready access to negative memories and emotions," just like Arbus, and "seem to have difficulty controlling the automatic spread of activation from one memory with a particularly negative tone to other, different negative emotions," also just like Arbus. This then suggests, according to attachment researchers, "the existence of an undifferentiated, chaotic emotional architecture," or what others have termed an "incoherence of mind."[9]

Attachment findings also show that securely attached individuals have better access to positive memories. As expected,

viduals have better access to positive memories. As expected, then, in Arbus's adolescent autobiography positive memories make at best rare appearances. Is this because they didn't exist, or because Arbus, in an atmosphere of incipient depression, foreclosed on sadness over good, happy, secure scenes? It's difficult to say. What *is* evident is what psychologists call "saliency units"—microscopic stories with an introduction, an action, and an outcome. Arbus wishes to act, to express her true desires, but is prevented from doing so, with the result being negative emotion. She wants to keep sleeping, but can't, is awakened, and the response is screaming, hate. She would like to explore the shantytown world, the reality closed off from her, but can't, with subsequent feelings of immunity and exemption. She longs for her governess to never leave her, so she cries in order to make her not go. She isn't satisfied. She's expected, because of who she is—the princess in a loathsome movie—to play a role she finds false and limiting. Like so many people, Arbus was contending with a split world. There was, on one hand, the opulence of wealth and the phoniness required to enact it and, on the other, the black ball of wool sitting on air, more real but also more frightening. One could not "see" the ball or go into it. For Arbus, the difficulty was to bring the two worlds together. It's not clear any blending was ever achieved. But splitting and integration is an obvious theme in Arbus's art, as evidenced by a lifelong fascination with twins and triplets.

Mamselle stands out as an obvious maternal figure. But what about Gertrude Nemerov, Arbus's actual mother? Where was she, and what was her role during Arbus's early life? First, it's important to get a sense of the complex household, the team of help around her. There were two maids, a handsome chauffeur named Scott, a cook, a German nanny (Helvis) for Howard, and Mamselle, Diane's governess (along with several others). Arbus's biographer Patricia Bosworth describes Gertrude—nicknamed Buddy—as an imperious, beautiful woman. Renee speaks of feeling "enforcedly close to her. I actually did not like her. That's putting it mildly." The atmosphere in the home, according to Renee, was "controlling" and "oppressive."[10] On the average morning Gertrude drank coffee in bed, smoked cigarettes, made calls now and then, and planned the dinner menu with her cook, Eva. As the day wore on she might ask Scott to drive her to Russek's, where she browsed and occasionally tried on the latest styles. When Diane was a little older she tagged along, in her white gloves and patent-leather slippers, feeling "crummy." Gertrude notes how, on Mamselle's day off, Diane would cling to her just as she clung to Mamselle: "She'd never let go of my hand."[11] There is a sense, remarked on by others, of Gertrude's basic impenetrability—the gorgeous chain-smoker who ran the show. A friend says: "Gertrude was deep down very shy, a woman of few words."[12] One of Diane's playmates adds: "It was a proud, odd household . . . Not much communication, but reverberations. Mrs. Nemerov never stopped looking at herself in the mirror." Renee explains: "We were a family of silences."[13]

Aunts, uncles, and cousins commented on Diane's detachment, her moods, or on Howard's "dour terseness." Gertrude found herself apologizing for the kids' strangeness—their noses pressed in books. She had a hard time figuring out what they were talking about. She felt them growing ever more distant, to which David Nemerov replied: "They're my children, Buddy;

they take after me." Still, as Renee notes: "My daddy always loved me but he wasn't around much."[14]

On the surface, Diane and her girlfriends lived fairy-tale lives, surrounded by "kvelling Mamas" insisting how special they all were, how talented and blessed. We were "isolated" and spoiled, a friend recalls, brought up like terrifically "well-bred eighteenth-century English ladies," shuttled to lessons in dancing, painting, languages, art.[15] Orthodontia and nose jobs were commonplace occurrences, privation a rumor.

By 1938, when Diane was fifteen, Gertrude fell into a serious depression she couldn't shake. She tells biographer Patricia Bosworth, "I had everything in life a woman wants and I was miserable. I didn't know why. I simply could not communicate with my family. I felt my husband and children didn't love me and I couldn't love them. I stopped functioning. I was like a zombie."[16] A clawing feeling of weakness hung over her. Her husband and children were one unit, set apart, unreachable; she was excluded, submissive. Rumors emerged of David's philandering—yet another secret.

She consulted various doctors. Nobody seemed able to diagnose what was happening to her. At last she was told there was nothing wrong; she should continue living her life per usual. In other words, her struggles were dismissed, minimized. Real help was denied her. Then, on an ocean liner to Europe, she began meeting with another passenger, an analyst from Chicago. He was oily, she says, with piercing black eyes. He asked her typically probing questions about her sex life, which she found unnerving. All along she remained stolidly depressed, "absolutely choked, panicked. Because I could not define my depression."[17]

She stayed stuck through the summer and into the fall. Then slowly, very slowly, she came out of it, at least partially. But Diane, she noticed, "was concerned for me; she observed me during those painful months. We never talked about what was troubling me, of course."[18] The depression, too, was a sort of secret. A subject to be avoided. This must have been made all the more painful and confusing because Diane as a child was also depressed, her moodiness there from the beginning. "You couldn't miss it," Renee says.

A shot of Arbus's from 1969 portrays her position in her mother's psyche. It is of a woman on a park bench. Her hair is perfect; she's clearly a salon regular. She wears pearls and a brooch. She smiles, sort of, but with a puzzled look, as if questioning the photographer's motives, wondering why anyone would want to snap a picture of her. Arbus's head is visible in shadow across the woman's right shoulder, another instance of the "black ball sitting on air," the daughter trying to find a way in. In one way or another Arbus shot her mother's basic loneliness and isolation over and over in a succession of foils: older women alone in buses, at the counters of diners smoking, in hotel rooms reading the paper. Often they are wearing furs.

So there were Arbus's manifold secrets, and those kept by Mamselle and Gertrude. Arbus clung to both women, feared both would leave her. She also was left with an example, early in life, of a woman who had all she wanted and who was miserable, expected to continue gamely in her role of queen. The same falseness extended to David Nemerov, once described as someone who "smiled continuously in public." As an adult Arbus noted a "phoniness" about him, a need to maintain a "false front."[19] He had started at Russek's as a window dresser. His skill at promotion led to the transformation of the store: He added a beauty parlor, a bridal salon, a boutique devoted to lingerie. He made clever copies of Paris originals—knockoffs. He okayed all merchandise, all ad copy, all window displays. With money, however, he was apparently hopeless. Figures bored him. A Russek's accountant paid all the household bills. Stories suggest that when he wanted cash, he would simply scrawl "$50" on a piece of paper and hand it to a Russek's cashier.

Patricia Bosworth concludes that David Nemerov "showed little warmth or interest in his children."[20] Renee agrees, although she became his favorite near the end of his life: "Diane and Howard used to poke fun at him, but there we were different. My brother called him a horse's ass. I never felt that way."[21] Neither Gertrude nor the kids saw much of him—he worked as many as fourteen hours per day, fighting to keep the business alive. In or out of the office he chain-smoked, like Gertrude, and suffered from a nervous stomach. He did not drive. He went everywhere by limousine. Howard Nemerov offers the following capsule summary: "He was an overtly powerful, power-using sort of guy. Diane and I were rarely punished, but everything in our house was based on approval, not love. This made us feel rather helpless because we never knew whether Daddy would approve or disapprove of something we said."[22]

One talent was giving advice. Arbus says he was "fantastic" at it. People sought him out for an opinion, for guidance. Interestingly, he betrayed confidences too, as when he told a girl's parents that she was no longer a virgin, much to her lasting despair.

Like many children, Arbus fantasized incest. She had the sense that her father preferred her to her mother, so cut off, depressed, miserable. A friend recalls the two of them flirting "outrageously." It's hard to know what to make of these facts. David did apparently recognize Diane's specialness. He wondered whether she might be too gifted for a little girl. Perhaps his affinity for her ran deeper than for his own wife. Perhaps he sought a closeness that was missing elsewhere, an intimacy denied him in other respects. No direct evidence exists for actual—rather than fantasized—incest, notwithstanding Arbus's penchant for referring repeatedly to secrets and "naughty" behavior when discussing herself and her art, or her sister Renee's comment ("We were a family of silences"), which implies a great many things unsaid.

Diane did hear about her father's constant philandering, though. A chauffeur claimed to have driven him to various assignations. Some suggest he even became romantically involved with Joan Crawford.

All told, there were four significant figures in Arbus's early life, each of whom helped set an emotional tone: her father and mother, Mamselle, and her brother, Howard Nemerov (Renee and Diane grew closer only as adults). Both Diane and Howard were gifted. Both went on to successful artistic careers, Howard as a poet. Creativity brought them into each other's orbits; they were, in a very deep way, simpatico. Their parents being relatively distant, they turned to each other for mirroring. Patricia Bosworth sees them as "twins" in the sense that they seemed unconsciously aligned; each knew what the other was thinking and feeling.

In *Journal of the Fictive Life*, an outrageously free-associative book about his own creativity, Howard talks only a little about his relationship with Diane, but even so, what he *does* say is especially important. Most of the time he can't be sure if what he recalls is fact or fantasy. The prose reads like a virtual transcript of a psychoanalysis. For instance, he speaks of feeling "neglected" after the birth of his sister—"no one telling me anything"—yet is not certain which sister the memory relates to, Diane or Renee.[23] Other recollections are more prosaic, superficial. A scar on Diane's face is traced back to the struggle over a doll that broke in their hands, the same doll Diane referenced in her autobiography fragment. The two played football in the living room—a perfectly normal sort of activity for two small kids—but got found out when the ball left traces of its nose and seam on the ceiling.[24] One Christmas morning Howard and Diane knocked over the tree, then secretly placed it back on its stand. Howard dutifully connects these three memories to a theme of guilt and "stealth."[25] He also thinks back on a portrait of Diane and himself, "on a red settee, wherein the artist's difficulty with perspective made us appear to have shoed stumps instead of feet."[26] He says: "Perhaps it was looking at that likeness of myself, seeing myself as a stranger, a mystery, that represented the secret beginnings of my art, that mystery which brings me now to *search the self in a spirit of guilt and isolation and some secrecy*"—a description that could easily apply to his sister's art as well. "Or else," he continues, "there is some meaningful episode belonging to the portrait, which I am unable to bring back because it represents something I can't look at."[27] He wonders whether what we suppress is not so much disagreeable—Freud to the contrary—as guilt-provoking.

In the next chapter, Howard returns to the portrait. "What became of the girl and boy?" They sit together—she in a white dress on the spectator's left. She wears white pumps, he black patent-leather shoes. Her expression, Howard recalls, "is an indescribable compound of sullen and shy"; his is bolder, insolent, defensive. "No smiles," he concludes.[28]

In a later poem he finds a distorted allusion to this portrait; it ends with "considerable bitterness" toward parents and their arrangement of the children's fates:

> *These hold the future tightly reined,*
> *It shall be as they have ordained:*
> *The bridal bed already made,*
> *The crypt also richly arrayed.*[29]

He goes on to record "a little, a very little, sexual experimentation with my sister" that probably dates to early adolescence: "But that is not a new memory, and was never in fact really forgotten." It's possible, he adds, "that this memory merely covers something of the sort that happened much earlier, at the time of the portrait."[30] The last observation takes on added interest, of course, in light of Howard's earlier comment about suppressing something he can't look at, and about guilt. The adolescent sexual experimentation is also important. It seems implicated somehow in the naughty/secret theme both Howard and Diane zero in on repeatedly. It suggests, too, that Arbus may have discovered, quite early in her life, that sex was a means of securing attachment bonds, of getting emotional needs met. Sex, even with strangers, was something she sought compulsively as an adult, for what are likely identical reasons. It got her in to other's people's experiences. It made her wanted.

It's possible to compare the actual "three-dimensional standing portrait" reprinted in the book *Revelations* with Howard's analysis of it.[31] (I assume they are one and the same.) In fact, Howard and Diane stand instead of sit, and there seems to be no red settee, but otherwise Howard's recollection, which he questions himself, is accurate (save for the fact that the children hold hands, an interesting omission). The expressions are much as Howard recalls: He looks proud and content, Diane a little withheld.

In the end, the portrait associations draw to them an extended comparison of photography and writing that is notably cranky but illuminating. Howard admits his lack of attraction to photographs. He describes Arbus's pictures as "spectacular, shocking, dramatic," focused on "subjects perverse and queer," adding: "Thou shalt make no graven image" (a reference to the second commandment's proscription against idolatry, image worship rather than worship of the true Christ).[32] Implicit in photography, he says, is the guarantee of security. The existence is safely past, reduced to a flat surface. Howard compares the photograph to "looking through the keyhole at mother and father": "But it takes the curse off this, as well as punishing for the presumption of looking at all, by reducing the observed experience to a flat statement—I was there."[33] Then more than this: "It also pretends that the camera fiend saw no dread secret but, after all, only the Eiffel Tower."[34] Looking at life without the mysterious amulet—camera, worn round the neck—would be "somewhat dangerous." The camera, he continues, pries into secrets, wants everything exposed and developed; it wants to know. But the trouble is, the knowledge it promises is "dialectically determined to be unsatisfying, so that there can be no end to the taking of pictures."[35] Everything known becomes an object, not what anyone really wanted to know, hence forgotten in the illusory thrill of taking the next picture. Photography is to guilt what writing is to innocence, since language constantly asserts reality to be "secret." He concludes by recalling that he and his sister used to blame each other a lot, get each other into trouble. His analysis of photography, he notices, "may well be another such attempt."[36]

So where does all this leave us? What does it say about the beginnings of Arbus's psychological life, the origins of her appetite for looking, the place where her images came from?

Arbus was raised in an enormously wealthy family yet found this wealth despicable and humiliating, loathsome. She dreamed of throwing it all away giddily. She was a princess more inclined toward the role of evil stepsister. That she felt this way shows some contempt for her parents in particular and how they chose to live their lives, their notion of what was important. It also shows that she found the facade of wealth stifling, a fact to be undermined, exploded.

Then there is the omnipresence of secrets, silence, and guilt. Both Diane and Renee registered the fact of things unsaid, emotions unexpressed. As Diane's friend put it, there was an atmosphere of silence and silence's reverberations. Not surprisingly, Diane's art was mainly about secrets, and making the art was "naughty" and "perverse." She did not stop at finding secrets only in her parents or her family, though that is where they originated. She spread them thickly; they got displaced defensively, away from the source. Arbus felt a constant need to uncover, along with a sentiment that knowing had little to do with telling. What she knew was better shown than said. But if her brother was correct, then Diane's using the camera to pry into secrets meant no end to the taking of pictures. The "graven images" merely multiplied.

Arbus was drawn, she once explained, to a gap between intention and effect.[37] In her pictures she was after the moment between trying to look a particular way and the result of this trying. This, too, can be traced back to the family atmosphere, the cultivation of personae. It had all seemed so perfect, everyone getting exactly what they wanted. But at the core was misery, as Gertrude makes plain, or falseness, as Diane discerned in her father. What Arbus kept wishing for was something real and true she could depend on, an assurance of love, not love based on approval. A God in whom she could place her trust.

But genuine, clear expressions of love were in uncertain supply for Arbus early on, as they were for her brother and sister. She never knew where she could get it or how long it would last. In the moments she thought she found it, she latched on hard, crying and pleading in order to keep it around. At the same time, she was expected to deny her needs for adventure; for experience not carefully controlled, meagerly doled out; to be the opposite of who she really was, an explorer. As Howard explains, he and Diane were never certain when approval would be forthcoming. Obtaining it therefore required a certain amount of duplicitous shape-shifting. There is, on one hand, the as-if self (or shape-shifter), and, on the other, reality. Compliance requires a mask, the very thing Arbus in her art worked to expose. Dad was a masked man—a "phony"—interested chiefly in keeping up the facade while concealing his various dalliances; Mom was isolated, cold, depressed, a "zombie" unable to make significant inroads into the source of her melancholia. If Howard's analysis is on target, then both he and Diane used their art as a method of revelation. They maneuvered in the direction of the peephole, the secret. Yet they never saw what they needed to see. The camera flattened reality, reduced it to an object, clicked guiltily, then moved on to the next shot. Language left the secret intact. Or at least this is how Howard saw things.

A flood of negative emotion is obvious in Diane's early autobiographical writing. Some of those feelings come from attachment history and Arbus's attempts, mostly unsuccessful, to locate trusted and trusting allies among her childhood friends. Anger, frustration, hate—all make corrosive guest appearances. What is it that Arbus hated, exactly? What was the source of her frustration? Not being loved in the sense of being understood, being allowed to become who she naturally was. Or not being seen, not having her actual perspective mirrored back empathically. Howard, too, underscores his bitterness toward his parents—their heavy-handed arrangement of the children's fates, everything so depressingly preordained.

Bad feelings present problems. They don't just evaporate, they *agitate*, requiring transformation or displacement; they seek a proper gradient. In other words, the affect has to be redirected, its form or object converted, its true source obscured. One option for dealing with unpleasant feelings, especially early on when humiliation, anger, shame, and hate are difficult to easily contain inside, is a form of psychological defense called projection. Negative emotions get expelled, forced into objects (or, more commonly, people). The objects hold the badness—they personify it, keep it at arm's length, where it might be displaced again or at least neutralized. It is a simple matter to look at Arbus's art in this way. The queer, perverse pictures of freaks signified a queer, perverse household; the household as it existed in reality and in Arbus's own psychology. The pictures are a kind of symbolic revenge. Her mother's composed coldness and "anti-strange" attitude, the family's silence, the fake decorum—all of it got scorched in art that exposed the rolling undercurrents. The pictures restored the snuffed-out emotion by placing it in other people—people who did not want it or possess it. When subjects complained of having been "Arbused," what they were objecting to was being made to *look* like Arbus *felt*. Their expressions weren't their own, they were the photographer's. It was her secrets on display, not theirs.

Hate can cause projection; it also leads to splitting, another psychological defense against feeling. The bad and the good are kept far apart to protect the good from infiltration. Arbus adored freaks, her first subjects: so sincerely and unapologetically committed to who they were, audaciously unmasked. But she also loved bifurcations, little twin girls, one shiningly good, the other holding suppressed badness. These girls were identical, perfect look-alikes, one and the same person, but they were also opposites, partial assemblies, split selves that reminded her, Arbus said, of herself.

Three photos in particular drawn from Arbus's oeuvre seem to depict both her sense of exile and the choked silences and disconnection within her family, the secrets. The first is especially haunting. It is titled "A Flower Girl at a Wedding, Conn. 1964." The girl of the title figures to be around seven or so—roughly Arbus's age when she visited the Central Park reservoir cavity. She wears a flower tiara and what looks like a white lamb's-wool jacket with a skin interior. The jacket, at any rate, resembles a fur. She holds a ribboned wicker basket. Her eyes are dazed, slightly fearful; she seems to possess some special knowledge; she stares absently, abstractedly beyond the photographer, not so much at her. Thin arms of nearby bushes reach out at her from the left and from below. And the background, her mind's metaphorical content, is fog-shrouded, crepuscular, dotted with indistinct pines or cedars. The girl's glowing getup contrasts with the world outside. She is white, bright, carefully assembled; the world grows darker and more menacing by the second, the fog seemingly advancing from behind toward her feet. This girl is Arbus. To all appearances she looks to be the perfect picture of a lucky prepubescent, pretty and rich; but in her eyes we see the darkness. It's touched her, and she will disappear into it.

It's important to focus on the background. It isn't incidental. When discussing a line of trees in a different photograph, Marvin Israel emphasizes how they need to look like "a theatrical backdrop" that might roll forward over the lawn. The world is no haphazard accompaniment. It is meant to suggest a crouching danger.

Another shot externalizing Arbus's sense of herself as a small girl, and the feelings she was expressing with too little frequency, is 1962's "Penelope Tree in the Living Room." Where the flower girl looks chiefly stunned, Ms. Tree, who later became a model and the ultimate sixties "It" girl, seems on the verge of violence. She's livid, arms akimbo, bangs perfectly snipped, enraged apparently by the bad luck of being so spectacularly rich. The "flower girl" was Arbus, and so is Penelope Tree—just another side. Even the biographies match to a startling degree. Tree was rich, her father a confidant of Winston Churchill, her mother

an American socialite who represented the United States at the
United Nations and who famously predicted for herself a life
of "parties, people, and politics."[38] There were servants, butlers,
maids, cooks, chauffeurs. Mother was never around, Father was
secretly bisexual. Also like Diane, Penelope was "virtually ignored. It was a buttoned-up household; nothing was talked
about." It was "poor little rich girl," Tree says. "It really was. It
was a funny way to grow up—but the visuals were good."

Tree was thirteen when Arbus shot her for *Town & Country*
magazine. She can't recall how the two came into contact. "It
was torture," she remembers, "the whole thing. Now I know
why everyone in her pictures looks like they do—because they
have to spend three hours with Diane Arbus staring at them."[39]
It was a hot day in August. Tree was dressed in riding gear at
one point, though in the printed shot she wears a pleated skirt
and penny loafers and stands on an ornate rug just to the right
of a chandelier. "Now I know what she was trying to get," Tree
continues. "Spoilt rich kid looking absolutely desperate in her
native habitat."[40] In other words, what Arbus was trying to get
once again was *herself.* The shot is another in a long list of examples of Arbus working hard and at great length to coerce a
subject to act out a drama less her own than Arbus's.[41]

Another photograph achieving the same objective is "A Family
on Their Lawn One Sunday in Westchester, N.Y. 1968." As Arbus explains, for reasons that ought to make instant sense in light
of the foregoing: "I have been wanting to do families . . ." She
mentions running into a woman outrageously made-up, many
of her features—hair, eyelashes—lividly exaggerated. Arbus
learns she's from Westchester, or "Upper Suburbia." She imagines her married to a dress manufacturer. "I said I wanted to

photograph her with her husband and children . . . They are a fascinating family. I think all families are creepy in a way."[42] The fact that she imagines this woman to be the wife of a dress manufacturer draws in associations to her father, David Nemerov. And if all families are creepy, then they all possess secrets their facade belies. These secrets are faintly sick. The word *creepy* denotes not simple mysteriousness; it means a sensation of repugnance or fear, as of things crawling on one's skin.

The photo is in the family's yard. The blonde-haired woman lies on a chaise longue in a white swimsuit, her eyelashed eyes shut against the sun. She does not take anything in; she does not see. She is oblivious and self-contained. To her left is her husband, in shorts with a small white towel across his privates. He covers his eyes, as if also blocking the sun. He conveys a sense of embarrassment, his participation in the scene coerced. He does not wish to be included. Between the two is a round table with ashtray and other sundry items. The table suggests the couple's apartness. They are disconnected.

The yard behind the couple is littered with papers and assorted detritus. One can make out a teeter-totter, a swing, and, off to the left, a picnic table. Then there is a boy, the couple's son. He wears striped bathing trunks. He is bending over to look into a small plastic swimming pool, in effect flashing his behind. His parents do not see him, so he searches the water for his own reflection. He is alone. A mini-Narcissus, he is left to his own devices to discover who he is.

The trees in the background do appear to loom, as Israel felt they needed to. They gather like clouds, suggesting an imminent storm. They create a feeling of motion.

Graham Clarke independently reads this picture much as

I do. The lawn, he says, conveys a sense of "emptiness, sterility, and dislocation." The "looming" trees suggest a "haunting otherness." The atmosphere is "gloomy . . . depressing." The parents lie "separate and alone." The boy "plays alone and is turned away from his parents." Altogether, "an image of family relaxation seems to have been inverted and emerges as a psychological study of estrangement and loneliness."[43]

There are other shots of this family, ones Arbus did not print. An image is taken in the same location with all three kids present. The father this time wears striped pajamas; again, he looks unwilling, annoyed. His son sits across his lap. Another son twists shirtless in the background in a sort of karate pose. The mother holds her daughter.

It's easy to see why Arbus preferred the picture she printed. It is a powerful statement. These are parents who are deliberately blinded. They perform no mirroring function, so the boy must see himself into being, find his own reflected identity there in the pool of water.

So the concepts of projection and splitting make some sense of Arbus's psychological life, her manner of dealing with emotion, and her use of photographic subjects. Another conceptual framework that sheds light on Arbus's early experience is attachment theory, touched on briefly already. This particular model was initially articulated by psychoanalyst John Bowlby, refined by Mary Ainsworth, and extended into the realm of adulthood by researchers such as Phil Shaver and Mario Mikulincer. It centers on the fundamental and formative importance of relationships with significant others with whom we come to form, from infancy, either affectional or attachment bonds. The latter are critical. We attach most firmly and come to rely most urgently on people whom we turn to for comfort and emotional reassurance in times of distress. These people are of course typically our parents, but not exclusively. Attachment hierarchies form over time. One's parents might be at the top of the list, but siblings, grandparents, and others—in this case even governesses—can play important roles as well.

The goal of attachment is the regulation of emotion. We reduce fear, anxiety, anger, sadness, and emptiness by seeking out those who reliably respond to whatever needs emerge. This seeking-out takes the form of what is called proximity seeking: staying close to and maintaining a bond with attachment figures. In the small child, proximity seeking has literal meaning; in adults it can take the form of phone calls, texts, and other relatively symbolic forms of connecting. We evolve over time an attachment system, an internalized abstract working model that forms incrementally; it works like an implicit theory of self in relation to others, and includes sets of expectancies about how people are liable to react when we turn to them in times of need. Will they respond—will they be available, capable of soothing fear, or will they reject us, ignore us? In short, can we count on important others?

Threats to availability and responsiveness are continuously appraised at an unconscious level. The attachment system gets intermittently activated, and when that occurs different learned strategies emerge—to draw out desired responses from those we depend on, we do what our past tells us works. These responses, functional or dysfunctional, become habitual, overlearned behaviors. They comprise our particular, unique attachment style.

One can be *securely* attached, an optimal but relatively uncommon style. If secure, we know from our history that important others will be available and suitably responsive in times of need. One can be *anxiously* attached, prone to overestimating threats, on a sort of red alert, never quite sure others can be counted on, in a state of low-grade fear and uncertainty. Or one can be *avoidantly* attached, habitually turning away from others and minimizing threats defensively out of fear that approach—proximity seeking—will lead to rejection or hostility. By now an impressively massive amount of experimental research exists concerning the life outcomes of these three main styles. The degree to which these styles correlate with other personality constructs such as extraversion, neuroticism, and openness (to name just a few) is also clear. In simplest terms, if a person's attachment style can be assessed, the results of that assessment tell us a lot about that person's moods, tendencies, defenses, thinking patterns, and, most important, motives for relating with others.

Attachment is a life-span model. Patterns take shape in early childhood but extend into adulthood. They persist, determinative of adult feelings, needs, and behaviors. What Shaver and Mikulincer have convincingly shown is that anxiously attached children become *hyperactivating* adults; avoidant children become *deactivators*. What does this mean exactly? That adults who make use of hyperactivating attachment-related strategies intensify emotion as a means of eliciting responses; they sustain and exaggerate fear, sadness, anger, anxiety, and rage. They "up-regulate" threat appraisals. The smallest signs of rejection or even simple disinterest are magnified. Helplessness, neediness, and vulnerability get overemphasized because these, in the past, have worked to mobilize attention and care. Hyperactivators are chronically clingy, needy, emotionally labile, and supersensitive. Their demands on others are intense. They crave intimacy, flagrantly advertising negative emotion until they get it, and when they do get it, they fear letting go.

Deactivators are mirror opposites. They aim to block, suppress, or inhibit emotional states associated with threat-related thoughts or perceptions. For them, negative emotion signals weakness, so they simply do not feel: They practice obliviousness and they develop an exaggerrated self-reliance, a compulsive independence. They need no one (or so they claim). They are the expert avoiders of the world. They refuse to problem-solve (they deny all problems), they have a hard time evaluating emotions (no practice at it), and they come to doubt the general goodness of the world, since counting on others has only got them hurt.[44]

I prolong this particular segue into the nuts and bolts of theory for one key reason: Attachment is a powerful lens with which to zero in on Diane Arbus's psychological life. It's an ideal blueprint we can superimpose on the particulars of her sense of self and others. It does not tell us everything we need to know—nothing will do that—but it's a strikingly effective organizing superstructure on which to base some initial formulations.

One thing is plain: Arbus was anxiously attached. Her needs for emotional reassurance, what some call "refueling," were not reliably met. She had few safe havens. Her father was unavailable, absent; her mother not particularly responsive, or only intermittently so, unloving and unlovable; and with one exception, Mamselle, to whom Diane could turn only ambivalently ("I don't think she kissed me much," "She was very strict," "She always looked as if she had a very sad secret"), Arbus loathed her governesses. There was Howard, who likely was high on Arbus's attachment hierarchy, but given the sexual experimentation the two of them engaged in (its extent not entirely clear), Diane couldn't have gone to him for soothing without some element of ambivalence, confusion, or fear. It wasn't until Arbus turned fourteen that a clearly available and responsive love object arrived on the scene, as if by magic—her future husband, Allan Arbus. She loved him instantly and ferociously. He became her "swami." She glommed on with what must have been extreme relief; she decided immediately that he was the man she would someday marry. Finally, a person to help regulate her emotions; finally, someone who did not disappoint or dismiss or turn a blind eye.

Gertrude Nemerov recalls Diane's clinginess on Mamselle's days off: "She never let go of my hand." Diane remembers how she'd cry and threaten to "die" whenever Mamselle took vacation. These are textbook anxious, hyperactivating strategies. Anxious children learn that threats and clinginess work to elicit responses, to secure love and care; they rely on such measures, first as children, then later as adults. Clinginess is a *characteristic adaptation*—an evolved habitual reaction to anticipated threat. It activates automatically in moments of fear. It becomes a pattern.

Something else is clear: Arbus was not a deactivator, although she might have used deactivating strategies now and then. As a rule, deactivators don't cling; they do the opposite. They suppress and avoid. They maintain distance. Also, deactivators divert attention from negative emotion. Arbus focused it. There occurred, as we've seen, regular crankiness, screaming, anger, shame, guilt, humiliation. These are adaptations too. Their goal is to cause attachment figures to pay more attention. They are a signal; they loudly communicate distress and need. And from time to time they work, or else they would not persist. But their reinforcement—responsiveness—is intermittent, unreliable. Yet according to research, that only strengthens them. They grow resistant to extinction.

These hyperactivating strategies are glaringly apparent in Arbus's later adult life. They can be seen in her interactions with friends, lovers, photographic subjects, and even with her psycho-therapist Helen Boigon. Arbus lived in red alert; her neediness and vulnerability, her promiscuity and sexual adventurousness reeled others in, drew them close where she urgently needed them to be.

What does all this mean for Arbus's art? For one thing, she was fascinated by families. A recently published book focuses entirely on her "family albums," making the concept out to be the organizing focus of her artistic endeavors. Some of these subjects were real family members, bonded by blood, others more metaphorically so. Whatever the case, it's safe to say that the concept of family is a prominent theme in many of Arbus's pictures. She used her art to better understand what family meant, or to find, in other families, a mirror of her history of discord and disjuncture. It was a way of refining her experience, or simply getting it out. In fact, if one looks at the pictures more closely, a vital element impresses itself. Many of her "families"—real or not—are arranged to present a vision of "oneness," a fantasized, wished-for closeness that contrasted with Arbus's own biography. They are anxiously, almost suffocatingly close, wrapped around each other in virtual symbiosis. Take Ricky Nelson and his family, 1971, one of Arbus's last published pic-tures. They sit on their lawn, the shrubs in the background again providing a looming, dark, terminal border. The kids snuggle tightly in their parents' laps. A daughter sits behind her father, rising Athena-like out of his head, which her arms frame perfectly. They come across as one squirmy, undifferentiated mass of flesh, a triangular blob. Also, unlike the subjects in some of the other photos, they appear happy. There is no undercurrent of gloom. Nothing explodes the facade.

Arbus shot Dave Nelson and his family in a similar fashion; she wants the two photos to rhyme. In this case she places them all in bed, framed by the bedposts' spires. The kids sprawl across the bodies of the parents; the family, once again, is tangled. A dog can be glimpsed near the bed's foot. There is nothing particularly gripping about the shot (except, perhaps, for the fact of its setting, the bedroom, a place of secrets). It might have been taken by anyone. Yet again symbiosis is emphasized.

Both of the Nelson shots are notable for their lack of easy irony. No latent truths seem to surface. What comes across, instead, is a feeling of happy unison, undividedness—a feeling Arbus appears to have lacked utterly. We are treated to a sort of antidote for Arbus's own family system. Hyperactivation of the attachment system leads to a search for connectedness as a defense against the threat of separation and loss.

The sense is very different in other pictures, for instance "A Young Brooklyn Family Going for a Sunday Outing, N.Y.C. 1966." This shot mirrors Arbus's experience, rather than presenting its antithesis. The mother has a vacant look, staring off into the distance. She seems preoccupied. The father is mild, agreeable, a seemingly nice man. A bonneted baby flashes an accidental peace sign while cradled in her mother's arms. The son, holding the hand of his father, puts the lie to the whole tableau. He is walleyed, clutching—it appears—his penis. All is not right. If Arbus did in fact believe that all families were "creepy," then she made this unit symbolize that fact. Along with the baby, mother holds both a purse and, interestingly, a camera. Across an arm is what looks like a leopard-skin coat. The baby is merely another object; the mother radiates no warmth, provides little reassurance.

Couples are another Arbus theme, and they too always seem to be attaching themselves greedily, arms and legs overlapping, huddled together against the world, a self-protective unit, a fantasized "safe haven." Their security comes from their indissoluble oneness.

I return to the effects of attachment insecurities later. For now it is enough to mark the theme. Arbus tended to seek out others anxiously from a position of insecurity and fear of loss of love; her wish was for a sort of mollifying merger. Strategies evolved, early on, for keeping love objects close, preventing their separation. Indicators of disinterest were carefully monitored; they gave rise to negative emotion that spread across a range of possible memories.

A final question, also on the theme of relationships and their safety, concerns the dynamic of sexuality and guilt and, by extension, secrets. There is much to cover here. What we know at present comes mainly from the history offered by Howard Nemerov—that he and Diane engaged in experimentation. He is not sure if this experimentation was limited to early adolescence, or whether it took place before then as well, at the time of the portrait he describes. There are memories that he can't bring back, that he can't "look at." We don't know what they concern. We also don't know how innocuous what they concern may have been. Something did happen between the two siblings—a fact attested to by Arbus's psychiatrist, Helen Boigon—but what exactly, and with what results, is impossible to say.

Still, it's interesting the way Howard uses these memories as a springboard for characterizing the latent strategies behind Arbus's art. Photography, he says, is guilt-driven, compulsive. Everything must be exposed and developed, but in an atmosphere of sterility, of fake neutrality. This leaves the photographer in a frustrating position: She captures the image, but behaves as though nothing has really been seen. So the answer is more pictures, and the cycle repeats itself grimly. Late in her life Arbus spoke of how her pictures were not "doing it" for her anymore. Howard's analysis may signal one reason why. Sexuality was a constant theme of Arbus's work, but it was a theme of her life as well. She shot transvestites and prostitutes, porn sets, researchers of the erotic, couples in bed; she participated in orgies, tracked down strangers with whom to have sex. The work can be seen as a secret code, a dream image with heavy, overdetermined latent content. The secret needed to be confessed; in fact, the more of a secret it was, the stronger the need to confess it.

Chapter 3

FAIRY TALES FOR GROWN-UPS

A RBUS THE TRANSYLVANIAN princess needed a prince, a living God less hypothetical than the one she hoped to place her trust in when fashioning her motto, a God on earth rather than sky-bound. The burden of minor and long-thought-out secrets was too much; the sins piled up. Friends disappointed: They were fickle, untrustworthy. Diane's mother was checked out, deracinated by depression, her father distracted by work and furtive liaisons with movie stars. Renee was fun to play with but young, and Mamselle withheld, nurturing her own secret sad side. Howard provided some support. He and Diane were symbiotically entwined, according to most who knew them, both seeking approval, both guilty, both sensitive to the family's subtle undercurrents, to the gap between how things appeared and how they really were. But Howard was a brother, the "little" sexual experimentation confusing—whatever it amounted to exactly—leaving more guilt with which to contend, more sin. It's interesting: As adults Howard and Diane rarely referenced each other, even after each achieved success.

What they had, what they'd done, was too fragile, too uncertain; each made as if the other did not exist. There was a tacit agreement not to draw attention, a silent sharing of at least one secret.

Into this miasma, in 1937, strode Allan Arbus, whom Diane met when she was fourteen—while feeling "restless and impatient," according to Renee[1]—right around the time of the writing of her second autobiography. He was five years older, five years wiser, excitingly mature. And he carried with him a camera, the machinery that would later become Arbus's ticket out of one hell and into numberless others of her own choosing.

At the time Allan worked in the advertising department of Russek's. He and Diane saw each other on Saturdays for walks in the park or for tea. This alone didn't suffice, for they also met in secret—a concession, perhaps, to Arbus's young age. By this time Diane had settled on art as her major area of study at the Fieldston School, despite her misgivings. She spent time painting but nothing ever seemed to paint as well as she knew it. She also disliked the "squishy" sound and feel of paint itself.[2] In 1939, at age sixteen, Arbus was selected for a senior English seminar along with nine or ten other students. An assignment was to write brief essays on classics like *The Canterbury Tales* and *Don Quixote*. Her reactions attest to the staying power of certain psychological themes. Chaucer, for instance, was calm and tender "because he was glad he was himself."[3] What she discerns in him is something she wished she had, a secure identity, a sedateness. He lacked her own "frenzied need for companionship," thus his comfort around the twenty-nine pilgrims.[4] Another thing appealing to Arbus is Chaucer's reluctance to detail any standard of conduct. He does not judge. To him, each person is a unique miracle. Arbus's response to *Don Quixote* is likewise preoccupied with self and others. Quixote she sees as "out of tempo with the world," his madness a way of "being himself to the limit."[5] He shook off convention, thrust himself in the world's face defiantly "because he was what he was, and he felt that was good enough." Arbus obviously found comfort in the audaciousness of Quixote's in-your-face qualities; she took a similar approach when it came to the making of photographs. She out-Quixoted Quixote.

Allan's solidity was the perfect poultice for Diane's thwarted needs. Here at last was a true attachment object, available, responsive, steady, strong enough in himself to absorb and hold all those sins, small and large, Arbus needed to declare. Allan was an ideal secrets container. And Diane clamped down hard and instantly. He was, moreover, the most beautiful man she had ever seen. Shortly after meeting him, she announced to her stunned parents—at the age of fourteen, no less—that she wanted to marry him, right away. They said no, of course. They also took steps to discourage the young couple, in one instance suggesting to the parents of an eighteen-year-old boy that they get their son to take Diane out. He did. He was captivated, as were many others—boys Diane dated out of a sense of duty, to placate her parents. "I used to stand outside her apartment looking up at her window, hoping I'd get a glimpse of her," one such boy recalls. "When you were with her, she made you feel like you were the only person in the world." As it happened, the eighteen-year-old recruit played the role of beard. He'd say he was taking Diane to the movies, then drive her directly to Allan.

Renee, according to Patricia Bosworth, saw Allan as "the

most important person in Diane's life, the crucial relationship."
She'd "never been that close to anyone before," except for Howard.[6] He became her "guide, her mentor, her reason for being."
He called her "girl," she called him "swami."[7] His word was
gospel. Salesladies at Russek's noticed Diane wore Allan's un-
derpants when she came in to try on clothes, as "a sign of love."[8]
Renee recalls tremendous amounts of "yearning and frustration," late nights of long kissing in the pitch-black kitchen. Allan
was tender, according to friends, but also "dominating."[9] He'd
tell Diane, "finish your sentences, girl," an attempt to curtail
her native abstractedness and dreaminess, her loosely associated
and tangential habits of thought.

Another thing Allan did was focus Diane's attention on her
own body, her physical self. He taught her breast and stomach
exercises, and she passed his advice on to others; she also suggested girlfriends stop wearing bras or girdles or deodorant
and go "natural" instead, funky body odor and all.[10] Her shame
slowly diminished. She stopped denying her "sensual animal"
self. She also, in keeping with the essence of this agenda, began
experimenting with masturbation. After everyone in the house
had fallen asleep, she would lock herself in the bathroom, turn
on the light, and "undress slowly in full view of the neighbors."[11] Then she caressed herself, aware others were watching.
She told a friend she did this night after night, with apparent
abandon, for several years. Howard called masturbation "worship" and approached it with a feeling of "religious guilt and
seriousness"; once, his father caught him in the act and told
him he'd kill him if it ever happened again.[12] Diane never was
caught, but she felt the same guilt, maybe for the same reasons,
yet now she tried defeating it with deliberate, self-prescribed

exhibitionism. It's another instance of her counterphobic tendencies. She undid fear by facing it, deepening it, until it spent itself. She scared herself fearless.

David Nemerov's opposition to this heated union, to the idea of an older boy Svengali who so obviously took his place in Diane's psychology, was profound and strangely excessive, transparently Oedipal. He never stopped fabricating scenarios that might lead to a breakup. He carped at, criticized, and mocked the couple endlessly, according to Bosworth. Once he gave Diane the gift of a little fur coat all the girls were wearing but she refused it—the "final blow," according to Renee.[13] Then, to enforce a cooling, he packed Diane off to the Cummington School of Arts in July 1938. There she met Alex Eliot, a "beaming wunderkind" with manic intensity who chainsmoked and never stopped talking.[14] He was nineteen—Allan was twenty—and the great-grandson of Charles W. Eliot, president of Harvard. As most boys did, he fell for Diane instantly, finding her "elusive," an "enchantress."[15] He rhapsodized about her lustrous hair, her black outfits, her strong calves, her mysterious intuitions. She told him all about Allan, including the plans for marriage, but he was already too far gone, entranced beyond reach or repair. She was the first great love of his life. The two took long walks, discussed and made art—the bond deepened. At one point Diane apparently asked Eliot, "Is it evil that I want both you and Allan?"[16] It's a startling admission. David's scheme apparently worked—to a degree. It got Diane thinking about other boys, sidetracked her fixation on Allan. The fact that she fell, a little, for Eliot, while she was still so fiercely devoted to the idea of eternally being Allan's "girl" shows yet again how intense was Arbus's need for closeness, for intimacy,

for the return of affection and attention. It was a need predating Allan, a need Allan certainly met too, but apparently not
uniquely. The need was bigger than any one person. Still, to
this point at least, there was no romance. Diane saw Eliot mainly
as a brother, a Howard surrogate. She wanted him, but she resisted acting on that want sexually. Plus, over the next several
years, Eliot got to know Allan too, a man in many ways his exact opposite: Eliot did everything to excess, Allan practiced
moderation.

Three years later, and less than one month after her eigh-
teenth birthday, Diane and Allan wed, just as Diane always insisted they would. Given her father's intense misgivings, this
was an act of clear defiance, a rejection of parental influence, a
declaration of independence. Allan gave her a Graflex camera;
they used their bath as a darkroom, both exploring the medium's
potential. When they made a picture they liked, they couldn't
go to sleep. They'd stay up all night looking at it. "We were just
two terrified, totally uninformed, wildly enthusiastic photographers," Allan says.[17]

In short order David Nemerov caved in to what was now
reality and hired the pair to conceptualize and photograph
Russek's ads. Arbus dreamed up arresting shots and posed the
models; it was Allan who took the pictures. But Diane was
shooting too. There were nude studies using herself as subject.
In 1942 Allan joined the Army; he was assigned to the photography division of the Signal Corps. In 1944 he shipped out to
India; Diane, pregnant with Doon, moved into her parents' Park
Avenue apartment.

The baby arrived in April 1945, with Allan away. Doon's birth
was Diane's entirely private experience, another secret moment.

She slipped away to New York Hospital the night before, leaving her parents a note saying, "I've gone to have my baby . . . Since I can't have Allan I don't want anyone."[18] She finds herself simply staring at the child, she tells Alfred Stieglitz. She expects to register sudden connection but doesn't. "I feel in such an odd, separate way about her."[19] Though pressured in her parents' apartment and having occasional trouble with breast-feeding, she was attentive, full of adoration for Doon, ribboning her bassinet with fresh flowers, posting cards on it of Roman ruins and English landscapes.[20]

After Allan's return, the couple worked through the late 1940s, expanding their client base. There was always the Russek's account, but they also shot for *Glamour*, *Vogue*, and *Seventeen*, including occasional covers. These were the magazines the two "thirsted" for, and as Diane says, "after it had rained like we needed it to . . . and the picture was going to be used . . . then the next day was like a miracle, gratis."[21] The work helped Arbus hone her craft and sensibility, her feeling for composition, but fashion as subject, as business, increasingly left Diane frustrated, artistically ungratified. Fashion was facade, making things look pretty—prettier than they really were—selling a dream. It was a proliferation of falseness, phoniness, a masking of reality. It was all "front," precisely what Arbus deplored when she saw it in her father, a very "frontal person," perpetually checking his look in the mirror. Always Arbus had her own native, intuitive sense of what a fact was. She knew it when she saw it. These facts were purely subjective, but they were *her* facts, what she alone saw. And they weren't pretty. They had no sheen. They weren't deliberately manufactured. She called them "stains," reality's residue, visual proofs of being. What Arbus detested more than anything was the mask. Masks were more unreality, more silence. They guarded the secrets she wanted out so badly. She was after not more phoniness but an antidote. Beauty itself was an aberration, she realized later, but others didn't see it that way. She was being paid not to; she composed ideals. So her first independent pitch to *Esquire* inverted the formula. Fashion was its own grotesque, seen in the proper light. Now she settled on the real thing, fashion's perfect antithesis. Eccentrics, weirdos, human extremes, human oddities—those things that weren't seen, weren't said, weren't avowed took her, camera ready, into additional shantytown worlds, this time without any hand-holding governess. The freaks she found or made "out there" matched the freaky world inside. It was a perfect fit.

A subject an artist latches on to first can become determinative. It sets a trajectory difficult to displace, especially when the work is successful and, because of that, a signature, as weirdos were for Arbus. One feels obliged to ride the wave. "Freaks" was Diane's initially consuming photographic obsession, her first wave, one she never stopped riding. And it became the leitmotif of her life and art—human pincushions, albino sword swallowers, nudists, dwarves, swingers, transvestites, the Backwards Man. She took buses to traveling-circus sites. She prowled parks where histrionic teens furtively tripped, or fought, or preened. She talked her way into the bedrooms of random lesbians and whores. She loitered in the vicinity of blind beggars, Jesus lovers, rabid feminists. In some essential way, Arbus *is* freaks. It's impossible now to think her name and not picture, in quick succession, a farrago of freak images. She succeeded in cornering the freak market, although she's hardly the first or last photographer to make grotesques a prime subject. She didn't seem to care much what variety of freak the freak was, so long as he or she was a "born freak" (sincere, authentic) rather than a "made freak." Made freaks annoyed her, left her unmoved; they were more phoniness, more artificiality. But born freaks were, as Arbus put it, "a very beautiful thing . . . They seemed like a kind of aristocracy."[22] Typically these were strangers she met, usually without introduction, and diligently, sometimes annoyingly pursued until they sat for her. Until, in short, she simply wore them down.

Jack Dracula, one of her very first subjects, is a model example. He got his name because of a talent for imitating Bela Lugosi. Rumors circulated that he slept in a coffin. He didn't. Initially he had "no intention of becoming a circus sideshow attraction." Arbus bumped into him, and before he knew it "she followed me all over the damn place. Wherever I was she'd pop up . . . She did the poor mouth routine—'This is how I make my living and I can't help it.' "[23] Arbus eventually got the shots she wanted and published them, somewhat to Dracula's surprise. She was nothing if not persistent. Few people managed to fend her off. The force of her personality was irrepressible: She was a genius seducer. She had a magic wand for working people. The clincher, apparently, was that Arbus bought Dracula lunch. His final verdict is interesting and a little surprising: "She had no personality whatsoever." This is a comment to set on simmer.

The Dracula scenario is vintage Arbus. Here was a "freak," audacious and oversexed (by his account) and lividly tattooed, whom Arbus managed to conquer through guile and tenacity. These human oddities, out of tempo with the world—like Quixote—mad, themselves to the limit, never failed to leave

Arbus utterly enthralled. To her they were larger than life, their uniqueness miraculous, like the twenty-nine pilgrims. She couldn't stop staring. The obvious question, the *core* question for any assessment of her life and art, is why. What did she see in these human oddities, or as she put it, the "anomalies, the quixotic, the dedicated, who believe in the impossible, who make their mark on themselves, who-if-you-were-going-to-meet-them-for-the-first-time-would-have-no-need-for-a-carnation-in-their-buttonhole?"[24]

We can start where interpreters usually do: by asking what Arbus *said* about shooting freaks. How did she make sense of it to herself?

What's clear is that she adored these subjects and in some way always identified with them, recognized them. That's key. They were partly her, like all her subjects were. She saw herself in them, and in shooting them, chasing them down and fixing them in static images, they mirrored something essential back to her that was reassuring—apartness, isolation, anomalousness, but also resolve. Overprivileged children of tycoons and freaks. Both were "toomuchblessed," in Arbus's romantic imagination.[25] The blessing was a burden to live with and through. "Privileged exiles"—Arbus coined the phrase to capture her subjects, but it fit her, too. She threw herself out of the land she belonged in. It's easy to see how overprivileged children are too much blessed, harder to see in freaks. But it made no difference for Diane. Just as she clamped down hard on Allan, who met her needs ideally, she clamped down on freaks as a liberating subject matter she joined with.

In no time freaks became an obsession; while mulling over

plans for work on freaks in the late 1950s, at the same time taking a second photography course with Lisette Model, Arbus filled three notebooks with various ideas. The ideas, in fact, never stopped coming; she was always in search of a new freak angle, a new disturbing or obscene subject matter—porn sets, anatomical deformities, S&M dungeons. On the brink of what was to be a substantial photographic assignment ("The Full Circle," published in *Harper's Bazaar* in November 1961), she records feeling "alternated haunted and blessed," in a "queer empty excited state."[26] Freaks, in implicit outsider unity, were a quasi-family. Arbus formed lasting relationships with a number of the people whom she managed to track down, such as Eddie Carmel, "the Jewish Giant." It wasn't enough for Arbus simply to get a picture. She needed *penetration*—of her subjects' lives, their way of being in the world. The pursuit was more than a little aggressive. She merged with their experience; she became a part of that experience. She formed intense affectional bonds that lasted years.

A question is whether, or how often, these bonds included sex. It's impossible to say for sure. (The role played by sexual motives in Arbus's work is explored in a later chapter.) My feeling, based on what is known about a few of her contacts with non-freak subjects, is that her art was strongly *sexualized*, a term used in reference to Arbus by her psychiatrist, Helen Boigon. So one element in play with respect to Arbus's work in the freaks vein emerges just as forcefully in her other work too: a search for closeness, affection, a need to find others who gave themselves to her and allowed her to exert some control over her fraught emotional experience, always tenuously managed at best. Arbus sought union with comforting objects. Freaks were no exception. Taking pictures, especially good ones, required intimacy. Arbus herself required intimacy, more even than Allan provided. It shored her up. It met a need only ever temporarily sated.

And this was a need *not* usually met by her family, either—chronically aloof, silent, inward peering, difficult to trust. But with freaks, Arbus belonged; she joined the club. Tod Browning's film *Freaks*, released by MGM in 1932 but quickly pulled from distribution only to resurface decades later, apparently bewitched Arbus mightily. She watched it over and over. And what she saw, apart from the deeply spooky "born" freak actors paraded improbably across the screen, was family—or a better, stronger, paradoxically normal family. We meet, for one thing, with several of Arbus's later subject types: a sword swallower, Siamese twins, a bearded lady, "the Living Torso," and a person who is half man, half woman. And we learn how freaks are an indivisible, tenaciously loyal unit, never to be broken. These misshapen misfits obey a very strict code of ethics: offend one freak, offend them all. When the film's villain, a "big" trapeze lady called Cleopatra, toys with the affections of a midget in order to get at his inheritance (she and her behemoth boyfriend plot to murder the dwarf), the freaks sit in grim judgment, united in their sense of betrayal. They rise as one, and through some sort of contrived magic succeed in turning Cleopatra into a chicken. The reversal is foreshadowed by the dwarf's scathing accusation: "Dirty slimy freak." Who are we asked to side with? Freaks, of course, the truly moral family unit. Who is fraudulent? The big lady and her "normal" conspirators. Freaks could be trusted. They'd never let you down. They were there when you needed them most.

One odd constant in Arbus's reflections on the freaks work is her tendency to equate the doing of it with the "perverse." In a thirty-minute audio recording of a lecture she gave shortly before her death, Arbus restates this point again and again.[27] The lecture itself sounds completely unrehearsed and freewheeling, more or less off-the-cuff. The audience erupts with laughter at regular intervals, though sometimes it's hard to guess why. Arbus comes through as whimsical, funny, loosely associated— almost *dissociated*—and surprisingly candid. She says whatever comes to mind. In fact, as the talk begins, she coyly confesses how she never knows what she is going to say at such events. It's all the more revealing, then, that from the very outset she emphasizes how her work, when she first started doing it, seemed so unmistakably "naughty" to her. As if she was doing something she wasn't supposed to do. As if she was getting away with something taboo, like, as she puts it, stealing into the kitchen for Oreo cookies. She wishes she could explain it, she says, sounding honestly nonplused. "I guess I've forgotten how naughty it was. It was a dirty thing to do. It was slightly unfair." She traces the work to a drive she can't deny. It is natural and irrepressible and somehow "comforting." And it signals freedom to her, the freedom to go places and to do things she had always been told she couldn't or, more to the point, *shouldn't*.[28]

It's the shantytown visit all over again, Arbus's prototypical scene—the small rich girl being bad but through her badness opening her eyes to the reality of suppressed worlds.[29] The art was a reaction against privation. The aim was to offend, and through that offense to make her secrets public, while at the same time keeping them, because of the shock value of the pictures themselves, at least partially concealed. She had it both ways, in other words. The pictures were thoroughly about her but not about her at the same time. She was a freak, but she wasn't a freak in the same way as the people she shot.

It must have come as a shock to her family, no doubt, to see her move in the late 1950s from fashion photography, a clearly acceptable enterprise that she pursued along with her husband Allan, to scores of shots of circus performers and freak-show centerpieces. Her mother has said that she could not understand Arbus's work. That comes as no surprise. It must have made little sense, considering the family climate of silence. Besides, Arbus was misbehaving. The work was a rejection of family; freaks were a new family, a confederacy she giddily joined. In a letter from 1965, Arbus responded to Howard's unfriendly characterization of her subject matter. She sounds hurt, though she tries distancing herself. She felt "pointed at," she says, when Howard's list of her themes came to read like a "dirty catalogue."[30] She notes a "temporary exemption" he grants her— which he really doesn't—from what he says about photography in general, and writes "not so hilarious" in the letter's margin. Someone else's take on her themes, their obvious perversity, she finds strangely surprising.

The words *naughty* and *dirty,* which she repeats almost bemusedly, are interesting choices. Adults aren't naughty, children are. They get called naughty when they misbehave. That single word seems to shoulder a lot of psychological freight. It suggests a motive that goes back in time. The need to be naughty that the pictures (and Arbus's description of them) confirm is an infantile need. It tells us that Arbus's motives, at least in part, arise out of childhood conflict. Again, the sense is that she was exploring experiences through her work that had been denied her as a young girl and beyond. For instance, she notes repeated visits to carnivals, "where I had never been when I was supposed to have been there" (i.e., as a child).[31] Most likely she invested the freaks with more fearsomeness than they actually possessed, even while saying she adored and loved them. This was an intention about which I believe she was relatively conscious: the effort to subject herself to perceptions she was not sure she could take. In fact, it is through doing exactly this—trespassing boundaries—that one grows as an artist. "Freaks," then, was a way of saying: no limits.

Maybe to tone down the fear of what she was doing or to make her motives appear less prurient—or both—Arbus also idealized freaks to what some, for instance the writer Joseph Mitchell, with whom she confided, considered an embarrassing degree. She imagined them as legendary, mythical, superpowerful, and, probably most important, fearless. "Freaks were a kind of movie star," she proposes. They were both anonymous and famous. They existed in a netherworld that you could not break into. "Everyone goes through existence with a kind of anxiety because there's some test coming. Freaks had already survived a supreme test and that gave them a kind of glamour."[32] With the pictures as proof, and by forming relationships with her freaks, Arbus succeeded in breaking into this weirdly elite fraternity composed of heroic personages, all of whom presented a riddle. She answered it.

What did it feel like to pursue this work? The best guess is that it felt guilty. It was a perversion, after all; it was something Arbus was getting away with. She felt two-faced about the whole enterprise. She pursued her subjects ferociously, manipulating them into sitting for her, not taking no for an answer. But all photographers of people do that, to some degree. Arbus's deeper, older, more infantile guilt—*not* common to all photographers—is another matter. It's far more personal. It's also far more inscrutable. It may have something to do with sexualization. And guilt accounts for the need to idealize and glorify and to make her subjects "singular" and awe-inspiring so as to fend off shame engendered by her truer motives. Freaks being Arbus's very first photographic calling suggests that she invested the work with all the resources available to her, conscious and unconscious, and wanted it to "say" everything she felt but had bottled up and denied.

In 1969 Arbus read Joanne Greenberg's fictionalized autobiography *I Never Promised You a Rose Garden*, about an adolescent in a mental hospital. One passage stuck out; Arbus went so far as to copy it into a notebook. Deborah, the girl confined, discusses cliques and groups and classes, the need to choose or be chosen, as with partners at camp or seatmates at school. What she discovers is that she can meet these demands of membership only with rejected outliers, "the disfigured, the strange, the going-insane."[33] Such alignments were never planned, never thought out, even secretly. They came intrinsically, in a way impossible to avoid or resist. Still, the "fragments" that had been drawn together "knew why in their hearts and hated themselves and their companions." Arbus too found the pull of freaks irresistible. If, like Deborah, she hated herself and them because of it, the pairing off was at least natural. She had no choice in the matter. These were the people with whom she belonged, like it or not.

So there was a lot going on inside Arbus that pushed her in the freaks direction, that made freaks an ideal vehicle for registering feelings and conflicts metaphorically. As prelude to this fresh development, and one additional component of Diane's emerging independence as a person and artist, she and Allan separated in August 1959, just as the freaks idea took off. The estate's book *Revelations* gives no reason for the break. It records it, then moves disjointedly along in the timeline. But as far back as 1948 there was conflict and drama galore. That summer Alex Eliot joined Allan and Diane at Martha's Vineyard; with him came his wife Anne, a "fashionable, high-strung blonde" who had been psychoanalyzed for her depressions and who once was engaged to the poet Robert Lowell.[34] The visit itself was not new. The couples got together a lot, knew each other well, everyone aiming for some kind of "artistic breakthrough."[35] One evening Alex Eliot read the group a chapter from his nascent novel. The response was silence. Then Anne erupted bizarrely: "Disgusting! Terrible! You are totally untalented."[36] It isn't known what, exactly, provoked this extreme denunciation, but whatever the case, Anne vacated the island later that night. Eliot was understandably devastated. The next morning he threw himself into the ocean, and though not, he says, suicidal, he swam too far and barely avoided drowning. That evening, alone on the beach, Diane "tender and maternal,"[37] according to Eliot, the two made love, a fact Diane immediately confessed to Allan. Weeks later Anne confronted her, but Diane wouldn't apologize. What she did wasn't wrong, she said. "She believed in trying to practice freedom," Bosworth says, "and unpossessiveness."[38] For his part Allan never discussed the affair. In Eliot's words, "when the three of us were together, it was almost as if it didn't exist."[39] But it did. It happened.

Years later Allan had his own romance. He'd set photography

aside, leaving it to Diane, whom he always knew had more promise, more vision and originality, and turned to theater. A serious
crush on a fellow acting-class student emerged; Allan got distant,
preoccupied, started wearing his hair wild and curly, the actress
telling him how "terrific" it looked.[40] Now Diane felt betrayed.
She didn't mind sex; what she feared was Allan falling in love,
withholding his affection and attention, directing it elsewhere.
She feared, in other words, the loss of attachment. "I am going
to be numbed!" she cried to a friend, rocking and moaning and
sighing.[41]

Allan's infatuation was the culmination of a slow period of
estrangement. It was decided Diane would move out—with
Doon and Amy, born five years earlier, in 1954—to a converted
carriage house in Greenwich Village. She still shared Allan's
darkroom, and the family met occasionally for Sunday break-
fasts. Allan maintained his financial support—the Nemerovs, for
their part, never gave the couple any money directly; while Allan
acted, he kept on at the fashion photography. It wasn't his pas-
sion, but it was a job, a way of earning an income. The news of
the separation Allan and Diane kept secret for three years. When
she finally told her parents, she records their reaction as "hys-
terical," ranging from "poignant" to "revolting."[42]

The Allan attachment in jeopardy, it was now all photography, all the time, a compulsive, emotionally distracting picture
taking. Another monumental influence, in a sense operating more
externally, was Arbus's relationship with her first and most influential mentor, the photographer Lisette Model. Model's effect
on Arbus's aesthetic and on her understanding of the nature and
process of taking pictures was profound. But beyond that, Model
proved the possibilities of freaks as a subject matter. Arbus's art

took shape in the way it did because of the kinds of things Model taught her and showed her. And the affinity does not end with the art. In a startling number of respects, Model and Arbus appear to have lived essentially the same life. Model modeled for Arbus a way of being. The key difference—one that made *all* the difference in the end—concerns motive.

Model—best known for her picture of a crouched, obese, female bather in a one-piece, her hands on her knees—first started teaching photography classes at the New School in the early 1950s. She apparently had a winningly aphoristic style; students adored her. Arbus studied with her in the mid-1950s, when she was thirty-three or thirty-four. Before Model, according to Allan Arbus, nothing "clicked," but after her "there was no more hemming and hawing . . . [Diane] was ready to be a photographer and just needed a release—Model provided that release."[43] She also provided, in the details of her life, an astonishingly close replica of Arbus's own early experience.

Like Arbus, Model was a middle child born into fabulous wealth, with servants and tutors and a "fairy tale house" that has been called a "fantasy of lavish ornamentation."[44] Her father was Jewish; according to several close acquaintances, he molested Lisette and left her with a sense of a childhood that was "very difficult and at times intolerable," deeply traumatic.[45] To make matters worse, on the heels of World War I the family lost quite a bit of its money, just as Arbus's family's wealth was threatened, though less so, by the Great Depression. In the 1920s Model attended a private school for girls with a child-centered philosophy; at Ethical Culture, Arbus was exposed to the same basic philosophy, and it always left her with a "shaky" feeling—she distrusted the uniformly congratulatory responses of her teachers, who acted as if she could do nothing wrong. Model grew into a "solitary child with a compulsive interest in people."[46] She came to believe in living intuitively, rejecting any sort of rationalizing process. Ditto for Arbus, who had the sense that it was the image, not her, that pressed the shutter and tended to leave her feeling "gently clobbered" by it.

So the affinities were intense: immense wealth, trauma, a lonely childhood, secrets. All these provided points of identification for Diane. Then, too, there was the nature of the work, which suggests numerous additional affinities of both approach and subject matter. It was as if Arbus magically stumbled into meeting a person who showed her a path out of a promising but choked existence, a virtual way of being, of expressing authentic truth. Model was a significant turning point, or as Allan Arbus put it, a release.

In her work Model insisted on "a psychological connectedness between artist and subject," calling her pictures an examination of the "hidden face," the mask, and "anti-glamour," themes also instantly discernible in Arbus's photos devoted to unmasking and what she called "flaws."[47] Model flirted with fashion photography, but the work failed to bring out the best of her talents; it was a subject "with which she could find no possible connection."[48] Same for Arbus. According to Ann Thomas in her detailed study of Model's life and art for the National Gallery of Canada, Model presented the mundane world as "an opera filled with characters . . . richly attired and living out a drama."[49] Arbus, in her "Full Circle" spread in *Harper's Bazaar* in 1961, for which she also wrote the accompanying text, says of her subjects: "These are five singular people who appear like metaphors somewhere further out than we do, beckoned, not driven, invented by belief, author and hero of a real dream by which our own courage and cunning are tested and tried."[50] Arbus called freaks "Characters in a Fairy Tale for Grown-Ups."[51]

Model felt a special empathy for and took a great number of photographs of the blind. Arbus found the blind similarly captivating, figuring them relatively incapable of fakery, maskless. She spent hour upon hour shooting a blind, bearded giant named Moondog, son of an Episcopal minister.

What's apparent is that a simple sampling of Model's subjects almost precisely duplicates Arbus's, or vice versa: dwarves, female impersonators, the circus, lonely solitary women. It's all there. Arbus's obsessions weren't only hers. They were Model's first.

Eventually Model was introduced to Sammy's Bowery Follies, a sort of "poor man's Stork Club" where both down-and-out and well-heeled New Yorkers congregated. It teemed with characters, singers and performers, and also eccentric "regulars." She shot the place with relish, finding it an inspiration, full of photographic opportunity.[52] Arbus had her own Sammy's— Hubert's Dime Museum and Flea Circus—where she lingered endlessly and met up with subjects like Hezekiah Trambles, the Jungle Creep, who performed five times per day, and the dwarf Andrew Ratoucheff, famous for impersonations of Marilyn Monroe and Maurice Chevalier. In her time the people Model featured were called "grotesques." In fact, editors sometimes warned her "not to show too many exaggerated, grotesque types."[53] The only magazine that continued to respond to her work favorably was the same one that responded to Arbus's, *Harper's Bazaar*. She found it "very daring" of them to feature her, just as it was daring of them to feature Diane.[54]

It's more than a little interesting, as one compares the two artists, teacher and student, to discover how closely the lives and the work intersect. It isn't that Arbus was, so to speak, duplicating Model; but she was younger, less experienced, less sure of herself, not as clear in her objectives, and so she naturally looked to her mentor for examples of just what it meant to do photography, how to begin assembling a career and a striking métier. It's puzzling, in this light, to see the lengths to which Model in particular went to deny any influence. About her own work, even, she maintained that though people and art were sometimes important to her, they "never influenced her." She was *sui generis*. She automatically extends the same anxiety of influence to Arbus, saying: "Diane Arbus was the greatest student I ever had. Not only because she came out with great photographs. Diane Arbus was influenced by nobody—but I have never seen anybody study with this seriousness and dedication as she did."[55]

This turned out to be a case in which the fame of the student outstripped the fame of the teacher. As Ann Thomas notes, "to see Arbus's photographs grow out of, depart from, and in the end eclipse her own could not have been easy for Model."[56] Probably not. But that doesn't account for Model's later denials. The fact is, Model exaggerated the distance between her own work and Arbus's for different reasons altogether. In a word, she found Arbus's art *pathological*.

I want to be careful not to overstate the importance of a handful of negative or loaded remarks. On the other hand, who knew Arbus's motives or work better than her mentor? So when Model asserts, after attending Arbus's posthumous show, that "her illness was projected into every single photograph," that her "schizophrenia" was undeniable, that her art reflected a "neurotic" life, these comments deserve careful consideration.[57] The question is what Model meant by saying such things—what she had seen in the photos to suggest such conclusions.

The ideas are not particularly anomalous. Others said the same things, though less starkly, and reached the same conclusions. As early as 1980 Shelley Rice published a piece in *Artforum* magazine comparing Model's and Arbus's work and finding not commonalities but "essential differences."[58] What Rice sees in Arbus's pictures is precisely what Model did. Utterly unlike Arbus's, pictures by Model reflect an "intense humanism," according to Rice, an "insistent formalism," an orderly, "painterly," and "highly structured set of pictorial relationships."[59] Her "extreme" sitters take on the air of character actors "whose attributes are exaggerated into theatrical displays."[60] Also, in Rice's view, Model's vision is essentially optimistic, an affirmation of "an archetypal and yet infinitely varied human essence."[61]

As for Arbus, the case could not be more different. To Rice, a "sense of isolation" separates Arbus's work from Model's.[62] This was a quality that "grew from a very personal, very specific childhood trauma into a general vision of people's unbridgeable isolation from one another."[63] Rice sees a lack of trust in Arbus's gaze, the same distrust she felt as an adolescent, in fact; she calls her work "passive/aggressive," "manipulative."[64] The pictures do not penetrate but rest on the surface, negating the possibility of understanding another person's experience. (As Arbus herself put it, "it's impossible to get out of your own skin into somebody else's.") Also, the camera's chief function for Arbus is to amass, in Rice's opinion, vicarious lives from which she was protected, partly because of her class status: She was "free to come and go, to enter into and then pull back from" her freaks' lives while they were trapped either by birth or circumstance.[65] Arbus, Rice says, transformed all her subjects into "reflections of her own personal trauma," and "this insistent sameness suggests that Arbus's photographs are much more assertive of the artist's subjective point of view—and much more manipulative of the sitter's—than Model's."[66] The work is both "simplistic" and "naive," revealing the artist's "essential void."[67]

These are harsh judgments, and polemical for their time. One wonders whether Arbus's suicide pushed the analysis in certain respects, like an offstage whisper. At any rate, the piece caused commotion. Unsurprisingly, the Arbus estate rejected permissions requests to reproduce photos in the essay, as an accompanying long editorial note explains. But Rice was on to something. What she is implying, and what Model too finally said, is that Arbus's art was a *symptom*: of her psychological dislocation, her isolation, her alienation. What she sought, far more than anything else, was experience—perhaps to fill an original void. And she did what she needed to do to get it. Model's feeling is that most artists keep their neurotic life separate from the work; one does not always or necessarily predetermine the other. But for Arbus, this more common scenario did not obtain. The life, its neuroses, determined the work's disturbed direction. Because Arbus was traumatized, so were her sitters. Her sitters were made to show the same isolation, sadness, blankness, and confusion that she herself felt. They were troubled and so was she. Just like her, they had no idea who they were. They were stuck, the life sucked out of them.

Take, for instance, the signature image of a "Child with a Toy Hand Grenade in Central Park, N.Y.C. 1962." It is one of

Arbus's earlier pictures, arriving on the heels of other freaks studies, such as "The Full Circle." Here the contact sheet is revealing. What it shows is that most of the pictures, in fact all of them with the sole exception of the printed one, are forgettable takes. The kid mugs for the camera. He smiles and postures, jokes and shouts. He poses in front of a birdbath. He looks, that is, *normal*, a clowning child. But the photo Arbus kept belies this normality, undercuts it. Arbus was after the freak beneath the facade whether it was there or not. The kid's face contorts into an angry-seeming grimace. His suspender flap hangs off his shoulder. His empty left hand clutches arthritically. His bony knees bulge. Then behind him, exploding surreally out of his head, stands a blurry, disapproving mother or grandmother, his unconscious, in a sense, his maternal introjection—a stuffy, bewildered Gertrude. The woman hovers there perfectly; she seals the shot. No doubt Arbus was pleased with this serendipitous element. Meanwhile, off to the side can be glimpsed a separate blurry family, out for a stroll in the park. And in the photo's upper right corner, a tree branch intrudes, as if reaching down to pluck the boy from the sidewalk. The grenade in the boy's right hand is the final saliency. He's about to explode. And he's going to take the viewer with him.

It isn't common that Arbus's child sitters comment on their experiences long after the fact, although some got tracked down following the 2005 Arbus exhibition as journalists worked different angles. We now know the grenade boy's name. He was Colin Wood, who lives presently in Glendale, California, with a wife and two children. "I have to say, Arbus felt a special empathy with that kid—with me," Wood recalls. "My childhood was not a comfortable one. My mother and father split up when I was very young. I had asthma. I was alone in many ways. I was a troubled boy." He goes on: "There's a sadness in her that she also saw in me, this need, which was very big in me at the time, to be accepted and appreciated and paid attention to. I was not directed [by Arbus to pose], but there was a collusion of some kind. There's almost this 'is this what you want?' feeling on my face." Wood concludes, "Arbus sought out her own heart in people but she peeled away the wrong thing. As much as I find beauty and love and sympathy in what she did, I also think Arbus went down this pathway that brought her to an inconclusive place. What she ultimately found, I think, is nothing. When I look at her art, I see a woman who was misled in many ways by herself."[68]

Wondrously insightful remarks, to say the least. They dovetail perfectly with what both Rice and Model assert—the notion that Arbus's pictures "reflect her own personal trauma." She saw her sadness in Wood, the need to be paid attention to that was such a big part of Arbus's childhood experience as well. And it's true, Arbus *was* misled by herself, if what Wood means is that she made art mirroring her own angry need to toss bombs. Wood says Arbus found nothing, she came to an inconclusive place. The work was a magic mirror, but what it reflected back was the same hostile sadness Arbus hoped to escape. It confirmed what she'd prefer not to know, not to contend with. Arbus's art was not restitutive; it did not allow her to rise above and work through trauma. It tended to be defensive, a temporary expulsion of internal conflicts. As Model spelled out, Arbus's "pathology" can be seen all over her shots. If the work is a kind of lucid dream, then what it conveys is a distorted representation of blocked psychological needs.

There's another Arbus picture that reproduces Arbus's early trauma—the sense of disconnect and aloneness, the fear of disapproval. This one came much later, in 1970. It's called "A Jewish Giant at Home with His Parents in the Bronx, N.Y. 1970." The giant in question is Eddie Carmel, who died in 1972, just two years after the picture was taken. He was said to be eight feet nine inches tall, though other accounts list him as around seven foot seven. He had apparently shrunk six inches at the time of his death due to a condition called kyphoscoliosis. He worked primarily in carnival shows, where Arbus happened upon him, but also appeared in a few films, including 1962's *The Brain That Wouldn't Die*. His charming dream was to be the world's tallest comedian. According to Eddie's aunt, there came a day when Eddie was fifteen years old and, looking down at his oversized body, declared, sorrowfully, "I am a freak." At the same time, according to others who knew him, when anyone called him a freak directly, Eddie would cry. Milton Levine, who ran a sideshow called the World of Mirth, explains, "He didn't want to be what he was. Eddie was a sideshow attraction, and he knew he was more than that. But there was no way to express it, he was trapped. A normal healthy brain inside the body of a giant."[69]

Again there's a contact sheet to compare with the print itself, and again most of the shots are unexceptional: Eddie stands with his arms around his comparatively midget-looking parents, all three facing the photographer squarely. As in the case of Colin Wood, the only shot that differs is the one Arbus chose to print.

What Arbus said about Eddie and his family in 1968 is telling. She calls him tragic, trapped. He defends himself with corrosive wit. The parents are perfectly mediocre. Their son's carnival career is, to them, a source of shame, it offends a practiced need for orthodoxy. It pleases Arbus to picture Eddie blissfully crushing both mother and father. "They fight terribly in an utterly typical fashion which seems only exaggerated by their tragedy . . . Arrogant, anguished, even silly."[70] It's impossible not to notice how this description squares with Arbus's own experience of a repressive family that disapproves of its child's chosen profession, and the child's wish to "crush" them all. She once joked about being Jewish and rich and from a good family and running away from it all giddily. Eddie was not rich, but by pursuing a carnival career he certainly ran away.

In the printed shot, Eddie stands facing his parents, his head nearly touching the living room's ceiling. The lighting leaves stolid looming shadows behind all the principals. The father wears a suit and tie, the mother a housedress. She peers upward at Eddie as if interrogating a massively sized perceptual illusion. He looks like a perspective trick, a figure in an artificially tiny setting. Arbus says: "You know how every mother has nightmares when she's pregnant that her baby will be born a monster? I think I got that in the mother's face as she glares up at Eddie, thinking, 'Oh my God, no.'"[71] Eddie is the elephant in the living room. Arbus during her own childhood felt the same way. Eddie was a freak who wished more than anything else not to be a freak. He could not express who he really was because of his abnormal size—his body betrayed him with a terrible finality. Arbus faced the same dilemma: how to express herself authentically when the odds were stacked against her by a family history that prepared her for anything but a career shooting weirdos. She too was a sideshow spectacle. But then, as Rice explains—and this is of course a critical difference—no one ever called her a freak (though they may have questioned her sanity). She was free to leave the freak world whenever she wished to. The identification only went so far as she let it.

Was Arbus crazy? Are Model and Rice correct? Does the work prove her madness? It's a tricky subject. Photography's an adventitious art. Pictures surprise. They either magically coalesce into perfect form, with all sorts of unexpectedly happy elements, or they fall flat, go nowhere exciting. There's always a strong element of chance. As Arbus herself once said, "You never know. You're always sort of feeling your way . . . What comes out is not what you put in."[72] But there's choice, too. Photographers single out the shots that say something interesting. They winnow, as Arbus did with Colin Wood and Eddie Carmel. In her shots, Arbus sought the wound that mimicked her own interior. She was depressed from an early age; the shots are depressing, they do not uplift or inspire. They are hard to look at. She was angry, also from an early age; the shots threaten to explode. She was adrift, her family unreal, her place in it uncertain; her subjects convey aloneness, dislocation. They aren't in transit to someplace better. They don't move. It's not wrongheaded to call the work a symptom, pathological, schizophrenic, neurotic; but what it really is, after erasing pathography from the equation, is *expressive*. Arbus kept remaking herself, as all artists do. She was obsessed, as all good artists are and must be. She identified; but did she empathize? I don't believe so, not to

the degree most people think. That was Wood's point. She peeled
away the wrong thing. She wasn't finding other people's secret
selves; she was finding her own, over and over.

Something else Arbus thought she saw in freaks was a talent
for self-deletion. They did not want to be who they were, so
they became someone else. This was Arbus too. She rejected
the humiliated, immune, exempt rich girl, crafting an alternate
identity—huntress, adventurer, magic mirror for the grotesque
confederacy.

The people she zeroed in on for *Harper's Bazaar*'s 1961 "Full
Circle" spread were all reduced, in Arbus's lengthy text, to an
identical need for self-multiplication. They are metaphors that
call the inevitability of personality into question. One named
"the Prince" signs his work with a symbol and regards himself
as a "splinter" personality.[73] He makes pronouncements such as
these: "The facets of a man's life so vary, in a seeming and rapid
inconsistency, that he appears to live his life as a succession of
characters . . . and his innermost secrets are hidden in time—
to outsiders, the personal history of anyone is merely a legend,
imperfectly understood—and a fable believed . . ."[74] He considers himself the "rightful Hereditary claimant to the Throne of
the Byzantine Eastern Roman Empire," though he was born in
Oklahoma.[75]

Max Maxwell Landar, another living metaphor, has "become
Uncle Sam."[76] He wears a red-white-and-blue satin suit to adver-
tise himself, though at first he did so far more mundanely, on
behalf of barbershops, pen companies, extermination services. He
says he used to be a nobody, but now he's a somebody. "I am what

I call a Personality." When he's ready he expects to become Buffalo Bill, among other possibilities, for as he declares: "I could be other people . . . I am a phenomenon!"[77]

Then there is Cora Pratt, the Counterfeit Lady. Her ability, too, which she pursued with inspiration and cunning, is "becoming someone else."[78] Cora is really Polly Bushong. Years ago Polly purchased a "fine and monstrous row of real false teeth" and thereby adopted her preposterous double (i.e., Cora). This Cora-self has tweaked the mustaches of diplomats, mentioned unmentionables at Chase Bank, and caught trains to Boston "with a rubber scorpion perched on her bosom."[79] In other words, just like the Prince and Uncle Sam, what Polly is isn't enough. She can be herself and someone else too—"other people," as Sam put it—so that's what she does.

These legends, as Arbus romantically styled them, have erased themselves. Through force of will they became more than they were. They perfected alter-egos in which to deposit imagined alternate lives. Others were luckier, in a sense. They were *born* multiplied. This is where another fierce Arbus fascination comes in: her fixation on twins and triplets.

As early as 1950, when Arbus was twenty-seven, she manufactured a double exposure of her daughter Doon that eerily prefigures her famous shot of the New Jersey twin girls. The right-sided Doon is happy, smiling, content, excited; the left-sided unsmiling, grim, blank, bothered. In the same year "Full Circle" appeared, Arbus is on the lookout for what she calls an "eccentric event." Twin conventions come to mind; she seeks them out over the course of a decade, right up to her death. She reports feeling, for some reason, "very gloomy and scared," and asks: "Why do I feel so sad?"[80]

Fringe twins got Arbus particularly excited—those who were adult or elderly and more difficult to find than young ones. Also thrilling were "double twins": twins who married twins and lived in identical houses with identical furniture. Arbus collected twin lore and twin jokes, conducting numerous interviews over a roughly ten-year span. One tale concerns twin women shopping. As they try on clothes, one, Martha, wanders off, away from her sister. Not noticing this, her sister asks absentmindedly, "What do you think of the dress, Martha?" but finds she's talking to a dressing-room mirror. Arbus corresponded with several sets of adult twins and got to know them personally, as she did many of her subjects. One of her very last excursions was a twin convention in June 1971, a month before her suicide.

In 1963 Arbus shot "Triplets in Their Bedroom"; she also shot nudists, midgets, teenage couples, and three Puerto Rican women on the street, all with identical hairdos, all looking formidably hostile, as if they might collar Arbus and bounce her along the sidewalk. In light of their shared expression, it's not clear why, or if, they consented to being photographed at all. The triplet girls Arbus encountered even after the fact at a triplet convention in Palisades Park. The shot is, on first glance, prosaic. A lot of Arbus shots are like this; they require multiple viewings. Three girls arrange themselves on a single bed in the center of the frame and look directly at the camera. But what slowly registers as the eye lingers over the scene is the sense that, in fact, these are not three girls but one. They form a solid undifferentiated mass, a Cerberus on guard in Hades. (In mythology, the multiheaded hound prevents escape from hell; since the girls stare directly at Arbus, it's she—and the viewer too—who is trapped.) They share arms; their black skirts blend into a single lower torso. One has a difficult time imagining them disentangling themselves. They almost seem like Siamese triplets.

Though they dress identically, sleep in identical-looking beds, and wear identical white hair bands, their faces assert difference. There's the mature wise girl on the left, the vaguely irritated girl on the right, and the smiler in the middle. Arbus saw this detail too, and it's what makes the picture hers. It's one of the relatively rare instances in which Arbus's reaction to the shot is on record. "Triplets remind me of myself when I was an adolescent," she says. "Lined up in three images: daughter, sister, bad girl, with secret lusting fantasies, each with a tiny difference."[81] This remark is fascinating if only for its simple consistency. Again Arbus makes the link between her photographs and secrets, lust, and being "bad." The triplets express Arbus's multiple roles—daughter, sister, bad girl. Arbus is just like Uncle Sam. It's as if she too declares, "I could be other people." The work is a proliferation of self, a subdivision that's both separation—splintering—and symbiosis, identification.

In 1967 Arbus shot the similar "Identical Twins, Roselle, N.J.," one of her most self-defining pictures. It's on the cover of her 1972 posthumous retrospective *Aperture Monograph*. She used it to create postcards that advertised her 1967 *New Documents* show. It was also the one print she gave to her psychotherapist, Helen Boigon, who later sold it to help pay for her daughter's medical school. In the psychoanalytic tradition, a gift like this is a disguised admission. It is not accidental or meaningless. It's an invitation to be known. But Boigon, just like Arbus's mother Gertrude, was not at all moved by her work. It was a subject that did not come up during therapy. Boigon made no effort to interpret what the work seemed to be saying.

The book *Revelations* reproduces contact sheet number 4539 with three sets of identical twins, including the paradigmatic shot.[82] In each case the pairs of girls, roughly the same age, are dressed alike. The pictures are taken in the same location, too: a Knights of Columbus Hall. The ground is brick; there's a white wall behind. In several instances one girl has her eyes closed; a few shots are full-body, others upper torso only. One detail that applies consistently to the Roselle, N.J., twins is the difference in their facial expressions. In three of the six shots, including the one Arbus chose, the girl on the right is smiling, happy, while the girl on the left is relatively dour. She never smiles once (across all six takes).

The Roselle twins picture duplicates the shot of the triplets. Not only do they look a little alike, they also wear the same white hair bands. Plus, like the triplets and Arbus's 1950 double exposure of Doon, two selves exist in one genetic blueprint. The twins are identical opposites, Doon too; the triplets a kind of id, ego, superego. The twins are also symbiotically entwined; they seem to share an arm in the middle where the bodies come together as they stand close, side by side. If triplets reminded Arbus of herself, twins must have too, maybe even more so.

In the twins Arbus saw her sister Renee. They had Renee's eyes; she referred to them as "wonderful Renee twins."[83] On the other hand, Diane and Renee shared the same feeling of exile. "I grew up like the little girl in the attic," Renee says. But then, as Renee stated bluntly: "Diane was depressed and I'm not. I'm more like my father."[84]

Colin Wood was tracked down to reflect on how it felt to be Arbused. Years later so were the Roselle, N.J., twins, Colleen and Cathleen Wade. They recall nothing about the day. They still own the dresses, which are green, not black as they appear in the photograph. Arbus met the girls at a Christmas party for local twins and triplets where she snapped more than three hundred photos; their parents agreed to let them pose. Bob Wade, their father, seems regretful in retrospect (though he accepted the gift of an original print). "We thought it was the worst likeness of the twins we'd ever seen. I mean it resembles them, but we've always been baffled that she made them look ghostly. None of the other pictures we have of them looks anything like this."[85] Nor did most Arbus pictures. She saw what she wanted to see and snapped it; the result was autobiography, not biography.

Arbus's twin fetish went beyond genetics. She twinned even nontwins; she saw sameness in difference. In 1967 she photographed two girls in matching bathing suits in Coney Island. It's a strange and ugly shot. The girls, who seem to be in their early twenties, stand close together, their shoulders touching. As in the pictures of real twins, they share a center arm. They look reluctant, oppositional. Behind them is some kind of inlet in and around which men are working. It is difficult to tell what's going on. Another shot features a couple holding identical hot dogs, each with one bite taken. The man looks exhausted, the woman preoccupied by something off to the right. Yet again center arms blend. In the background a blurry tree trunk split-screens them.

Examples of the same sort of heightened sameness or simultaneous sameness-difference are easy to come by. Mutating Santas from a Santa Claus school are arrayed across a lawn. In a shot resembling the hot dog eaters, two ladies in an Automat, each in a hat, each with carefully drawn eyebrows, raise bracketing cigarettes between index and ring fingers. Albino sisters pose in front of a carnival tent. A blind couple lies in a bed in Queens. Arbus even twinned people and their pets (or proto-pets), as in the hilariously deadpan 1964 image of a lady bartender and her souvenir dog: The woman's florid white hair (or wig), belted in the middle with a tightly coiled braid, perfectly duplicates the fake toy poodle to the right of her.

Kafka, a writer Arbus read and admired, spoke of living "as if I were entirely certain of a second life." In her pictures Arbus constantly asserted the same possibility. She welded bodies symbiotically, forced physical unities, while at the same time flaunting binary oppositions. I see this as a visual representation of Arbus's internalized object relations. It was the way Arbus's mind was organized. Splitting, the unconscious separation of positive and negative feelings, is one of the earliest, most universal psychological defenses. It's a way we protect important love objects about whom we feel intensely ambivalent. The more anger, resentment, frustration, or hate, the more splitting. Splitting isolates the good, prevents permeation, keeps the bad at bay. For some people, those whose very early years included particularly frequent emotional privations, the bad grows badder, more powerful, more fearsome. The goal of integration is what the mind naturally works toward; it's a more mature, emotionally secure, realistic mind-set. The world is not black-and-white. The good is never all good, the bad never all bad. But integration can be risky. Joining feelings together and holding them in turbulent unison can be depressing. Only when good feelings outweigh bad can splitting be willingly relinquished.

This was Arbus's challenge. And it's a conflict that lent power to her art. We all use splitting, so we all locate aspects of our own psychology in the shots of twins and triplets. We are all, to different degrees, split selves. But what made splitting *especially* necessary for Arbus individually was her early life, a history that is *not* universal. For Arbus, there was a lot of anger and hate to keep sequestered, cordoned off. Good relationships were in relatively short supply, so good internal images of self and other remained fragile and vulnerable to spoilage. Bad feelings were split off self-protectively, but they and their accompanying imagery were also projected, making the world a sad, angry, freaky place. Arbus externalized the bad, lodged it in pictures that contained it temporarily until the process repeated itself. Success made Arbus feel queasy and "besieged." On one hand, this reaction is common to artists. They see the flaws in the work. Plus, finishing projects entails loss, and from there, depression. The process ends. And the ending of the process is a little death. But what made this all the more unnerving for Arbus was the fact that, in looking at her pictures, she was looking at her own exiled badness. She projected split-off anger, moved it from inside to outside, but then it never stopped staring; the art was a continuous reminder of all those things she denied and repressed. It was a dream, a *lucid* dream, but one insufficiently disguised. No wonder it made her feel besieged. Seeing it was to peer into a mirror that only ever told exact truth. And the truth was accusatory.

Colin Wood, the grenade boy, says Arbus found "nothing." I don't entirely agree. What she found in the pictures was a refinding—of what she had inside, what she expelled. It was dangerous. It was angry. And it was right on the verge of blowing up.

The symbiosis theme, bodies blending and fusing into one, implies a tentative, primitive movement in the direction of integration. But this was never accomplished. The bad was simply too abundant, the good too meager. Triplets reminded Arbus of herself and probably never stopped doing so. Her dividedness was ongoing. As late as 1969 she mentions reading R.D. Laing's *The Divided Self*, a phenomenologically oriented analysis of the structure of schizophrenic experience. Laing, she says, "seems so extraordinary in knowledge." She imagines doing "monologues by mad people under his guidance with his translations of the sense of what they were saying and my photographs or how they looked or behaved," but worries that the idea may be too "ambitious." She also wonders about potential "legal problems."[86]

It's worth considering how *The Divided Self* spoke to Arbus personally. To begin with, the book takes aim at what Laing calls the "false-self system," how one comes to be unembodied and ontologically insecure, as well as at "schizophrenogenic mothers" and "families" who bequeath to children a "death-in-life existence in a state approaching chaotic nonentity."[87] As Laing asks in a passage that could have been written expressly for Arbus: "What can happen if the mother's or the family's scheme of things does not match what the child can live and breathe in? The child then has to develop its own piercing vision and to be able to live by that . . . or else become mad."[88]

The ontologically insecure person adopts a falseness bordering on parody. His every mechanized move symbolizes exactly what he rejects—deadness. Clinging to the most tenuous of identities, he fears absorption (what Laing calls "engulfment") and loss of being should he risk relating with another person openly. Reality in its impingement is felt as "implosive"—it looms menacingly as in fever. And though dreading being turned into a thing by the reifying gaze of another, he fashions a preemptive "petrification" of personality as a means of self-protection. His aim is not gratification of self but self's preservation. This becomes, ironically, a matter of life and death. If he chooses a "death-in-life" existence, then at least he chooses it: The deadness is his, not a sentence imposed from without.

The book is filled with richly detailed case studies in the existential/phenomenological tradition, with careful attention paid to the structure of the patient's lived experience. Laing's aim, he says, is to show that the schizoid person can be understood, to find interpretable psychological meaning in what others regard, and dismiss, as mere "symptoms." Arbus doubtless saw herself in these people. She wasn't a schizophrenic, exactly, but she *was* divided.

There is James, for instance, one of Laing's pseudonymous patients: "Other people were necessary for his [literal] existence." Like Arbus, he lived a polarity between "complete isolation or complete merging of identity." There is Mrs. D: "She was very afraid that she was like her mother, whom she hated." Baffled and bewildered, nothing she did "had ever seemed to please her parents." She was "unable to discover, as she put it, 'what they wanted me to be.'"[89] Her parents were "completely unpredictable and unreliable in their expression of love or hatred, approval or disapproval."[90] Next is Peter, who made no difference in his parents' lives. They "simply treated him as though he wasn't there"; his mother "hardly noticed him at all."[91] The central issue for him had crystallized "in terms of being sincere or being a hypocrite; being genuine or playing a part."[92] As we've seen, Diane's parents were likewise essentially self-obsessed.

Her father "showed little warmth or interest in his children";[93] her mother "wanted her only to do the right thing, the correct thing."[94]

Then there is Mrs. R, another patient. Her parents, too, "were always too engrossed in each other for either of them to take notice of her."[95] She grew up wanting to fill this hole in her life, "to be important and significant to someone else," in contrast to her abiding memory of herself "as a child that did not really matter to her parents, that they neither loved nor hated, admired nor were ashamed of."[96] Eerily like Arbus, she was married at seventeen to the first man who really noticed her, finally feeling triumphant and self-confident under the warmth of her husband's affections. But then he left, and her panic returned. Laing concludes: "The pivotal point around which all her life is centered is her lack of ontological autonomy. If she is not in the actual presence of another person who knows her, or if she cannot succeed in evoking this person's presence in his absence, her sense of her own identity drains away from her. Her panic is at the fading away of her being."[97]

Laing concludes with the more deeply disturbed Julie, who felt "unreal," whose father had withdrawn himself emotionally, who was accepted only when she behaved falsely or "good" (i.e., as though existentially dead), and whose choice lay between merger/symbiosis and an alienating, parabolical madness. In the end Julie "splits" into what Laing calls "molar" units—partial assemblies or partial systems, each with their own stereotyped personality. Terrified of the intense anxiety occasioned by integration—the prospect of internal *folie a deux*—she sought refuge, instead, in "unrealness."[98]

All these cases mirror what we have already discovered in

Arbus: self-engrossed parents; a sense of unrealness; a distaste for masks, falseness, and fronts; fears of being alone and related needs for merger with others; a split self-image—in short, a "divided self." These were the pivotal points around which *her* life centered, to use Laing's terminology. And these central issues naturally found their way into her art; she sought her own "piercing vision," a picture of the world she could live with.[99]

Symbiosis also amounts to another hyperactivating attachment-related strategy. Arbus needed intimacy, and it didn't always matter much where she got it. Relationships lifted her up, compensated for early attachment-figure unresponsiveness. So the art revised history; it made a world of enforced closeness. People invaded each other's space, breached barriers, leaked into one another. As Arbus explained, "It's impossible to get out of your skin into somebody else's. And that's what all this is a little about."[100] It's a rueful admission. I don't think she ever accepted this impossibility. It's interesting that she *noted* it. The fact is, getting out of her skin and into somebody else's, lodging her own interior in others, is what Arbus was *constantly* up to. Her work is impossible to imagine otherwise.

What's a wonder is her rate of success getting in. Here's where Jack Dracula's observation comes in: "She had no personality whatsoever." Arbus was a shape changer. She had a gift for sensing what she needed to be to get what she wanted. And what she always wanted were two things, neither mutually exclusive: the shot and the person in the shot. She claims to have hated how she worked people, but her protests against herself aren't particularly believable. She never gave up the hunt. She was just too good at it. It was just too successful. So Dracula's right: To get into other people, to make them react, to make them *trust* enough to react, one had to be a bit of a zero. To get swingers, Arbus was a swinger; to get anguished little girls, Arbus showed her damaged side; to get sexologists, Arbus suggested sex; and to get freaks, Arbus interpolated the inner weirdo. This was more than artistic necessity. It was who Arbus was. It was the structure of her personality. Inside, no single central, stable self abided. So she drew on the multiplicity, relied on it, instinctively unveiled one or another side whenever necessary. Happily enough, doing so came naturally. Unhappily enough, when she got the shot, when the secrets had been confided and exchanged, she slipped back into the same lonely, unhappy place. And the antidote was more shots, more secrets, more intimacy. There was never any end that worked.

There's an interesting observation from Polly Bushong (aka Cora Pratt), one of Arbus's "freaks," demonstrating how important it was for Arbus that her sitters authentically stood in for her own experience. "Diane Arbus was awful nice to me. Sweet. She spent all day photographing me in the garden . . . But before she left she asked me a couple times was I really sincere about having these two people inside of myself? I kept telling her I was sincere, but I guess she didn't believe me . . . Actually, I didn't mind, because I don't see how you could label me a freak."[101]

She wasn't much of a freak. Arbus was.

Chapter 4

SHAME ERASING

T HE MID-1960S WAS a turbulent time for Arbus, in
some respects a transition period consisting of slight subject changes and important partings. In spring of 1963 her father,
a very heavy smoker, was hospitalized with lung cancer. It was
clear to the family that he was dying. He hallucinated scenes
connected with the business, imaginary pockets, papers he kept
trying to stash away, once even asking, according to Arbus's
notes, Who made the moon? He died on May 23. In a later interview with Studs Terkel, Arbus admits she did not adore him,
and also confesses guilt about the way she stood—"almost like a
creep"[1]—in the corner of the hospital room, spellbound by the
dying process, by her father's gradual diminishment. In an impulse to save the experience eternally, she photographed him, an
act she calls "really tremendously cold."[2] She says, ambivalently,
"I resent that implication"—her own implication, in fact—"but
I suppose there is something somewhat cold in me."[3]

The loss is freeing. In July Arbus visits her first nudist camp,
the so-called Sunshine Park in New Jersey. In February 1964,

she shoots Mardi Gras, and on the way home photographs the Queen of Burlesque, Blaze Starr, for *Esquire*. By this time her daughter Doon had left for Reed College in Portland, Oregon, a small liberal-arts school soon to be known nationally for its hippie vibe along with rampant student drug experimentation. A student of Howard's moved in to help with the care of nine-year-old Amy.

In 1965 the physical stimulus for so many of Arbus's reveries, Hubert's Museum, closed down. Arbus shot a handful of group portraits, the assembled freaks looking wistful and wan. In a kind of obituary for the place, she writes, "We had our shame and our awe in one gulp," then adds: "If you've ever talked to somebody with two heads you know they know something you don't."[4]

Freaks were what Arbus shot first and what she never stopped shooting. She *was* freaks, in the way repetitive subject matter tends to define an artist, to become that artist's thumbprint. In this Arbus is hardly alone. Writer Patricia Highsmith was the amoral murderer Ripley, whom she always referred to as though he was a real person and not a fiction. Flannery O'Connor was grotesques, the religion-mad, Bible-brained misfits dominating her stories, seeking their idiosyncratic redemptions. Philip Larkin was the misanthrope in the center of so much of his poetry; Hitchcock the falsely accused victim; Kafka the existential meaning seeker thrown into nothingness and ambiguity. It's not uncommon for artists to be governed by one endlessly clawing obsession that they rework in different forms and modes. It's a nucleus informing growth and future development. It's not exactly the sharp vertex of an inverted pyramid, but it's close. It seems at least partially implicated in everything the artist does.

Arbus is a perfect example because she shot hundreds of freaks.

If, over time, the simple predictability of their omnipresence bores us, it never bored her. She glamorized them, invested them with ominous subjective meaning. Her quest is heroic. The dark adit she enters is the unconscious. It's all very Orphean, but unlike Orpheus, she never looks back.

What is it about these pictures? Like Plath's *Ariel* poems, they are decidedly not nice. We do not enjoy being made to contend with them. Lucien Freud, in some respects a similar sort of artist committed to exposing the unseen, has spoken of his horror of the idyllic. Arbus shares the sentiment. The idyllic she considered more or less a cover-up, more falseness. Her photos therefore revel in ugliness. We are made to see, as if for the first time, all those things we sensed were there but could not locate on our own. Our terror is a little bit domesticated (if we're lucky). Then it's a matter of deciding what to do with these people— cross-dressers, midgets, albinos, giants. Do we condemn or assimilate them? Are they us or not us? Probably both. That is a realization to come to terms with. It is not easy. Arbus is not easy.

Another thing Arbus did, especially in her later years, was aim her lens and herself, like a heat-seeking missile, at sex. Arbus was freaks, no question. But in a number of respects, sex defines her motives and conflicts even more effectively. It's naughtier, for one thing; dirtier, at least potentially. If what Arbus wanted, and this is what she said herself, was to freeze sordidness, perversity, nastiness, puerility, then sex fits the bill. Freaks show us, aggressively, what we prefer overlooking, but sex ups the emotional ante. It also requires confrontations with intimacy and relationship, not to mention trust, all problematic subjects for Arbus from the age of fourteen at the very least. And sex is where our most guarded, most tremulously revealed secrets reside. Nothing got Arbus going like secrets—her own and her subjects'. The idea of secrets delighted and unnerved her. She couldn't live *with* them—felt the need to share them, get them out somehow, often at a price—and she couldn't live *without* them: They gave her something to relish, nurture, inflate. The secrets were a wondrously independent, split-off, mostly impenetrable second life playing itself out untouchably. The friction of having these secrets inside, some mean, some exceptional, led her to want to find them in others. The sharing turned her on. It was an energizer. It was a thrill, and it was a means of getting close.

All this being the case, it's strange to what slight degree sex gets focused on in biographical or critical writing about Arbus. It's there sometimes—Patricia Bosworth in her biography recounts assorted escapades—but it's marginalized, set aside, dislocated. We live in an age when sex hunkers around every corner, when books—such as the acutely odd and thoroughly flawed analysis of Lincoln's presumed homosexuality—positively reek of sex obsession. The Arbus literature? Not so much. It's almost sex-phobic. And while it's true that sex has almost nothing to do with many of Arbus's pictures, it is just as clear that a startlingly large amount of her work is sex-themed. These shots and the feelings that went into them, or that they elicited, are of critical importance. Together they tell a story—parts of which emerged during the two years of psychotherapy directly preceding her suicide—but one insufficiently aired.

Arbus's catalog is replete with pictures of cross-dressers, nudists, lesbians, porn sets, prostitutes, swingers, dominatrixes, and with legions of people, famous and not so, posed languorously across their beds. Yet what tends to get focused on, far more than the sexual element in all such images, is the eccentricity of the sitters, the way they seem to be juggling identities. But we simplify the pictures by singling out this quality of the grotesque. The oddness of the subjects obscures another equally pressing theme: of sex and sexual exploration, of dirtiness behind the scenes.

Take, for instance, an altogether unlikely example, the series of pictures of Ozzie and Harriet Nelson, among Arbus's final published shots. Three portraits of the Nelson family appeared in *Esquire* in June 1971, a month before Arbus's suicide. The freakishly normal is just as full of possibility for Arbus as the abnormally freakish. As she once put it, with statistical accuracy, beauty itself is an aberration. Normal portraiture, according to Robert Hughes, includes tacit agreements between artist and subject allowing the sitter to mask himself and project this mask—of success, of dignity, of beauty, of role—upon the world. But Arbus accepts no such agreement. She was always most interested in shooting that gap between intention and effect, freezing mobile moments between what Hughes calls reflection and self-projection. What results is a denuding. Arbus decomposes her subjects. With Ozzie and Harriet, her horror of the idyllic is in full display. Somehow she gets them, as she did so many of her subjects, to lie across their bed. This fact alone is worth noting. Arbus had a genius for getting people to do things they ordinarily found unsettling. How she did so is, as we've already said, a mystery. It had something to do with the force of her personality, her talent for eliciting trust. She was the mirror in which people saw things they never knew were there. Or they knew, they suspected, but denied, declaimed, ignored.

Ozzie, apparently attuned to Arbus's less than generous intentions, is unpleased. We sense his reluctance. Arbus captures him pre-pose. There's a sternness in his face to which we are unaccustomed. He wears a corduroy blazer and tie. Harriet, by contrast, is far more canny. She smiles, her head near Ozzie's shoulder. She looks unflappable. On the bedside table lie books and an alarm clock. The couple is framed by the rising, twin steeples of the bedposts. The shot resembles Arbus's 1963 picture of triplets in their bedroom: Just as the three girls seem to blend and fuse, so do Ozzie and Harriet. The Nelsons share a hand. Where does Ozzie end and Harriet begin? Are they one person or two? Arbus shot Dave Nelson and his family in precisely the same way. They, too, are in bed. They, too, are framed by the bedpost's spires. I was looking at the Ozzie and Harriet photograph in a show at the Portland Art Museum. Most people passed it by with little comment. Yet one woman saw what few others managed to. "It's hard to imagine Ozzie and Harriet having sex," she said. We are made, at least unconsciously, to ask what Ozzie and Harriet *do* in this bed. We fantasize a clandestine life. How much naughtiness has been transacted here?

A slightly "naughty" fantasy in itself, actually, especially since the Nelsons embodied the concept of a wholesome American existence. They epitomized the blandly conscientious, upright, happy family. (The *Esquire* piece's unsubtly ironic title was "The Happy, Happy, Happy Nelsons.") Their show lasted fourteen years on American TV. Ozzie has been called the "narrative linchpin" of the show (despite his basic fecklessness), Harriet the "wise homemaker." And if they are Dave and Ricky's parents—on TV and in reality—they are, or were, our parents too. They modeled our mostly wished-for reality. So when Arbus makes us see them in bed, and has them see us seeing them, we're placed face-to-face with the unexpected. We perceive what we repressed. Arbus foists the drama on us.

Sometimes the obvious gets missed; we ignore it, more intent on IDing arcana. One obvious fact of Arbus's body of work is this: She took an enormous number of pictures of people in bed. This can't have been anything but intentional. The examples are just too plentiful. A partial list includes William Mack, Sage of the Wilderness, and His Serene Highness, Prince Robert de Rohan Courtenay, both from *Harper's Bazaar,* 1961; Marcello Mastroianni in a hotel room, PLEASE DO NOT DISTURB sign dangling sedulously from the open door; the Jesus-besotted "Bishop," looking skyward and sitting beside a bejeweled cross; Mae West with a monkey; the triplets; the stunningly reposed Brenda Frazier, twenty-eight years post–Debutante of the Year; weight watcher Alice Madeiros, posing smilingly behind one of her old ballooning dresses; Kate Millet and Fumio Yoshimura; Mia Farrow in bra and slip skirt, knees pressed together demurely; a Puerto Rican housewife; a couple naked and kissing; a girl in a coat, her Camel pack beside her, ashtray full; Arbus's own father two weeks before he died of lung cancer; a girl in patterned stockings; two female friends at home; a seated transvestite with crossed ankles; a blind couple; a transvestite at her birthday party, wigged and grinning broadly; a woman in her negligee; a girl on her bed with her shirt off, exposing incipient breasts. Contact strips of the Mexican dwarf Lauro Morales also show him posed in various ways in bed. Arbus shot him on a number of occasions, including in his hotel room in 1970. He wears a hat. A white towel covers his privates. "I was photographing in a kind of amaze," Arbus recalls.[5]

Arbus asked for intimacy from her subjects—this was one of the hyperactivating strategies arising out of attachment insecurity—so getting them into bed makes perfect sense psychologically and artistically. She didn't want only to shoot these people, she wanted to know them and them to know her. She was a participant in their lives. If she sensed that anything essential was being concealed, if what they showed her was less than or different from what she wanted, she aggressively forced her way past the facade. It was a war against cliché (in the writer Martin Amis's words), against the idea of privacy. It was an invasion.

Feminist Germaine Greer (author of the *Female Eunuch*) described her own battle against an Arbus invasion that also took place, appropriately enough, in bed. It's a scene I return to later, as Greer did herself in a recent publication. To Greer, Arbus seemed at first a "rose-petal soft, delicate little girl" in safari jacket and short-cropped hair. She had hopped around photographing the author at a press conference in Sardi's, held to promote Greer's book. The two met up later in Greer's seedy Chelsea Hotel room on a hot, muggy day. Arbus "immediately" asked Greer to lie down. "I was tired," Greer says, "so I did what she told me." In an instant Arbus knelt on the bed and hung over Greer, shooting madly. "It was tyranny. Diane Arbus ended up straddling me . . . keening over my face . . . She kept asking me all sorts of personal questions, and I became aware that she would only shoot when my face was showing tension or concern or boredom or annoyance."[6] Greer naturally had her own ideas about how she wanted to come across, which Arbus deliberately rejected. What ensued was a "duel" over the image, a virtual wrestling match between two formidable opponents.

The only reason Greer did not tell Arbus to "fuck off" was because she was a woman. "If she'd been a man, I'd have kicked her in the balls." What Arbus said about the shot is informative. She mentions—this was also 1971, the same year as the Nelson photographs—doing a "lousy page for a terrible new magazine called *Newwoman*, of Germaine Greer, who was fun and terrific looking but I managed to make otherwise."[7] A lot of what Arbus was up to, it seems, was managing to make people look otherwise—other than how they wished to look, other than how people tended, on average, to see or imagine them. And for some central reason, Arbus must have felt that getting people into bed served her purposes uniquely. We don't typically see, for instance, Mae West in bed—with pet monkey, no less. That's an intimacy one tends to guard closely. But Arbus was a trespasser. She jumped the crime-scene tape.

Arbus peppered Greer with questions of an intimate nature while clicking away; the sexual aspect was obvious. Arbus was intrusive, assaultive, the session itself a sort of emotional date rape. Greer, as it happens, emerged victorious. The shot one sees reprinted was disappointingly tame—feminine and vulnerable (though other shots, recently for sale online, show a more agitated Greer). Arousal was what Arbus took from the encounter, the state she whipped herself into. She was turned on, and she used that feeling to intensify the making of the art—even though the page turned out lousier than hoped for.

In the mid-1960s Arbus began exploring the science of sex, intellectualizing what was in fact a conflicted emotional subject for her. She made contact with the Institute for Sexual Research, founded by Dr. Alfred Kinsey in 1947. She looked into the life and work of Dr. Hans Neufeldt, a pioneer in contraception and the founder of the *Journal of Sexual Research*. Neufeldt ran a successful gynecological clinic on Park Avenue that served patients until 1991. An influential "sexologist" with more than six hundred publications on birth control and sexual functioning, he championed a number of sex-related causes including homosexual rights and legalized abortion. Arbus also contacted Albert Ellis, author of *Sex Without Guilt*. Ellis invented a theory of therapy called RET, later renamed REBT—Rational Emotive Behavior therapy. The idea was that thought created emotion, that problematic feelings like shame or fear stemmed from irrational beliefs, dysfunctional cognitions. Therapy amounted to a restoration of rationality; flawed or morally absolutist thinking along the lines of "I should not be so promiscuous" got disputed, replaced by clearer, more logical trains of ideas. In short, Ellis advocated the triumph of thought over feeling. If we could learn to think more accurately about the things we did—things we had a hard time accepting—difficult emotions disappeared. There was a thrilling simplicity to what Ellis had to say. It's no different from what is now called Cognitive Behavior Therapy. For Arbus, the possibility of thinking shame away, cooling its heat with reason, must have been intriguing. It was a solution to be explored. Sex without guilt was what she was after, from the time she masturbated night after night in full view of neighbors; Ellis showed a way there—not that Arbus ever really arrived.

All this research translated into action; its meaning got worked out in the art, where Arbus always put theory into practice. She went in search of couples willing to pose nude; she also shot people in the act of sex. An instance of the latter is "Couple Under a Paper Lantern, N.Y.C. 1966." In fact, the lantern hangs down from the ceiling, hovering brightly above the heads of the lovers. It's the only light in the room, which is noticeably squalid, mangy. The carpet's beat-up and grimy with coins scattered across it. The walls are cracked and peeling. The bed has no frame, no headboard; it looks to be a mattress and box spring lying on the floor, clothes in a bundle to the right. No faces are visible; the couple kiss, the woman on top. Both are naked. The woman's hand blurs in its motion as she gives the man a hand job.

A different take on the same couple shows the greasy-haired man on top this time, kissing his partner. He's in a crouched position over her. His right knee digs a little painfully, one guesses, into her rib cage. He pins her to the bed.

Neither image achieves much eroticism, if that's what Arbus was after. There's an authenticity—something Arbus admired in certain porn shots—but the truth is ugly. No tenderness comes through at all. The sex is physicalized, minus any romance or sentiment. The setting establishes a context of filth that's superimposed on the sex act itself. It may be real—it actually happened as we see it thanks to Arbus, who was there, amazingly, to record it—but the result, for the viewer, is repulsion. What we see is the "stain" Arbus always talked about capturing.

Around the same time Arbus shot orgies, too, in which she was sometimes a "willing participant."[8] The art and the life merged. Pictures, after all, were only part of what she wanted out of the experience. A different idea was to snap her sex partners reposing "naked in the aftermath."[9] These shots don't exist in any published form, though it's hard to say. We don't know who may or may not have been a "partner." According to the estate, Arbus judged this effort a failure. The pictures lacked "eroticism and authenticity."[10] At any rate, it's an odd predilection. She's after a gallery of conquests. What she was hoping to see in the faces of these lovers, what she wanted them to show—what the "aftermath" consisted of—is anybody's guess.

There's a contact sheet, number 4457, from the book *Revelations* that comes with a punch. It's a relatively rare instance of the Arbus estate releasing something *genuinely* revelatory. Or, on the other hand, it's a tame confession standing in for others more scandalous and thus *not* shown. The subject is a mixed-race couple, the man African American, the woman possibly Latina. His pants are always on—across the nine takes—while she's in partial or full undress. He's usually shirtless. They sit on a couch in a typical living room, in front of a table with a crowded ashtray, funny suburban wallpaper behind them. In a few of the shots she smokes. Nothing very sexy is going on. They touch or kiss occasionally. He smiles and laughs a lot; he seems slightly self-conscious. In the frame second from the top of the center strip, Arbus appears, startlingly. We would not know this, not notice it, except for an accompanying caption: "Diane is lying across the man's lap in place of the woman."[11] That is, Arbus inserts herself where the man's lover had been. (Apparently it's the other woman who takes the shot.) Arbus is fully nude, lying on her left side, one breast partly visible, her right arm dropping to the floor. The man places his right hand gently atop Arbus's right thigh. He smiles broadly, looking directly at the camera. Arbus's eyes turn away, her face expressionless.

This shot is unique in Arbus's oeuvre. In no other published picture does she pose with a subject. There are no other nudes of Arbus, either, except for those few shots she took in 1945 of herself in a mirror pregnant, in white pregnancy underwear.

It's unexplained who these people are. We don't know if Arbus knew them personally or if, as with so many of her photographs, they were strangers she seduced into sitting. We also don't know if they were lovers—Arbus's lovers, that is. But given what she was up to in the mid-1960s, prying into sex as both scientific and photographic subject, throwing herself into experiences with obvious determination, on a virtual mission, it's unlikely Arbus's role was confined to photographer. Lying nude in a man's lap suggests intimacy of some sort, at the very least. And to suppose Arbus was part of a threesome, for instance, is no major stretch. The shots may even depict the so-called aftermath of sex. Whatever the case, it's not the only instance in which Arbus shot a couple yet found herself wanting more than pictures. She's pushing her boundaries. She's investigating artistically and emotionally what it means to be sexually free—of guilt, shame, judgment, in the way Albert Ellis described in his book. Free love was the zeitgeist. Arbus wasn't alone in exploring it. But sex is the ultimate secret, and for her, secrets were everything. She used the pretense of picture taking to redefine herself sexually. She opened up to the arousal the pictures induced and acted on it.

This pattern continued for several years. Perhaps the feelings never cooled at all. In October 1968, for instance, she tracked down self-described "erotologists" Phyllis and Eberhard Kronhausen,[12] experts in human sexuality like Neufeldt and Kinsey. She knew of their books, including *Erotic Art*, *The Sexually Responsive Woman*, and *Pornography and the Law*. Eberhard Kronhausen can't recall exactly how he and his wife came to meet up with Arbus. Most likely a mutual friend passed along a phone number. The couple had just arrived in New York from California and were staying in a friend's vacant apartment. Arbus had an obsession with swingers, according to Kronhausen, to go along with her orgy and sex-act fascinations. So did he and Phyllis. They had engaged in participant research on the topic, both in the U.S. and Europe. They were the real deal. An idea was to shoot them before getting up in the morning—a method aimed at increasing authenticity. Arbus, in fact, planned an entire photo series devoted to couples in bed.

The Kronhausens were ideal subjects, or so it seemed. They were, in the argot of the times, sexually liberated. Nudity unnerved them not in the least. They were game. They were experienced. Several of Arbus's other acquaintances declined a similar overture, feeling—a few of them—uncomfortable with their bodies, uptight in their skin. This was never an issue for the Kronhausens.

The couple agreed to an appointment. Arbus was to arrive in the morning, at around seven A.M. Without any ado, Diane arranged her tripod and camera. Since the Kronhausens did not sleep in the nude at the time, there was no disrobing. They simply behaved as they always did before getting dressed and preparing for the day.

Phyllis recalls Arbus with her back toward the bedroom's large bay window overlooking the East River. She was positioned left of center—from the Kronhausens' perspective—her camera pointing at the head of the bed. The couple reclined in a white comforter. Phyllis was most likely wearing a short nightie, Eberhard pajama pants. Neither recalls the exact conversation, but according to Eberhard, it was centered on sex, since that was Arbus's keenest enthusiasm.

Before a single shot was taken, Arbus suddenly straightened

up, looked directly at the Kronhausens, and declared, "I can't photograph." Initially it was difficult to figure out what she meant. Everything had been proceeding uneventfully.

The Kronhausens wondered what the difficulty was.

"To our complete surprise, she said: 'I am too excited. I want to get into bed and make love with you.'"

Despite their immensely varied sexual experiences, the Kronhausens were bewildered. Not, in fact, in the mood for any sort of sexual adventure, they offered whatever excuses came to mind, and suggested the three have breakfast. Over coffee and bagels, Arbus did what she so often did with her subjects: She told secrets. She had been shooting other couples, she said, several of them self-described swingers, and the sessions had sometimes ended up in bed. On different occasions, Arbus revealed, she had participated in group sex.

The three parted, agreeing that Arbus would return, leaving the question of sex for a later date and time. Many months later Phyllis and Arbus talked for several hours. On that occasion the Kronhausens were staying in the home of a famous female movie star. Phyllis suggested introducing Arbus to this woman, but she showed no interest. It's true—Arbus had always been "very little drawn to photographing people that are known." The minute they go public, she said, "I become terribly blank about them."[13]

Arbus's suicide left the Kronhausens regretful: "We did not realize, at the time, that Diane was in such dire psychological straits." As it happened, no photos ever got taken. Others have suggested the Kronhausens shared with Arbus assorted pictures of actual penises, all culled from their sexual research. Eberhard denies that. He *may* have shown Diane illustrations, he said, given her taste for the bizarre—photos of Japanese dildos, penises made from tortoiseshell or polished wood and stone. "We were interested in artistic representations of anything sexual, not in anatomy!" Arbus, of course, was interested in both.

It's an oddly sweet and almost sentimental plan for a photo series: to get couples in bed in the morning as they first awake. Bed is a safe place, a sanctuary. It is where we shake off the day's residue. Sometimes we don't want to leave it.

Subjects waking in bed are in a pure and vulnerable state, transitioning between sleep and wakefulness. Bed is a twilight zone: We aren't unconscious, we aren't fully conscious. What we *are* is preconscious, on a borderline. Arbus may have worked this out theoretically; it may have had something to do with why she kept taking the same sorts of bedroom photos. It was a refinement of her ideas. Subjects waking in bed exist in that gap she always wished to capture: They are pre-effect, pre-mask. As the Kronhausens suggested, this is a poseless state, a state of authenticity. In her sex shots Arbus was also after the authentic and the erotic—yet she was finding the combination hard to freeze in decisive moments.

Sleep's also an infantile state, including regressions to psychotic, primordial modes of thinking. In sleep we become pure involuntary brain function. This brain function produces dreams: visual hallucinations. These dreams defy logic, time, rationality. The ego, as Freud once put it, lets down its guard. The unconscious rushes forth. In bed, as in play, or art, or decompensation, we are most like children. We move through waking from childhood to adulthood. Arbus wanted to record this movement, to see what it looked like—to shoot the borderline.

But then, most obviously of all, bed is the site of sex. It is where we liberate a secret side, where the secrets expose themselves. It contains a hidden history almost never uttered. The fact that Arbus's sexual feelings interfered with her picture taking in this instance raises a number of interesting questions. Her work required seduction. She had to get people to drop control, to share what is usually most guarded. Arbus worked from awkwardness. She did not like to arrange things. "If I stand in front of something, instead of arranging it, I arrange myself."[14] She moved from dyscontrol to control. In the process of composing herself, she composed the image. The image—reality, a subject—always prevailed, however. "I never have taken a picture I've intended. They're always better or worse. You're always sort of feeling your way."[15]

Getting to this place, this constantly shifting ground, called for a basic hypocrisy that Arbus found annoying. But the seducer occasionally gets seduced. Arbus claims that all her manipulation and ingratiation, the phony oohing and aahing she did, never meant anything like "in my private life I want to kiss you,"[16] but that is precisely the feeling the Kronhausens elicited. She *did* want to kiss them. Arbus lost control, or relinquished it intentionally. She said so. And this time, unlike others, the shoot stopped.

Why didn't she use the arousal to make the picture? The world of sexual feeling and the world of imagination are intimately connected. The vision has a sexual quality; its intensity, specificity, urgency, and obsessiveness spell that out clearly. Several of Arbus's sessions with swingers ended in bed, as did the orgy sessions. On those occasions she made the art, then acted on the feelings the art evoked. It was all one intoxicating gestalt. The Kronhausens, for some reason, provoked a different kind of conflict. Or at least they simply said no.

The decisive factor might be control. As with Greer—as with all Arbus's subjects, in fact—the fight was over the image. We want the artist to interpret us. We want her opinion. But we do not like the mirror showing something we prefer not to see. There has to be recognition. Arbus demanded the supreme license. She negotiated, but only to a point. Once she made it *in*, she brought out what *she* wanted. She assumed control in a context of dyscontrol. Control, however, was exactly what she could not assert with the Kronhausens. She was too excited. She was not able, this time, to arrange herself. She became the subject. It would have been the Kronhausens' picture, so she did not take it.

It's impossible now to say how often Arbus faced this dilemma. On the other hand, by shooting sex in so many different ways, from porn sets to orgies to apartments to hotel bedrooms, she threw herself into a dynamic with the potential for all sorts of complications, especially in light of her own life history. One rarely hears of Arbus finding herself unable to shoot. She almost never seems stymied. The sense, in fact, is of one enormous and frighteningly encompassing roving eyeball click-clicking away indefatigably. That's what makes this single encounter so beguiling. What began as a typical Arbus trespass ended incredibly prosaically—with coffee and bagels.

In her subjects, Arbus always recognized herself; there was always that oneness, the blending and fusion. Seeing who they were and what they were doing in the deepest way possible was a means of finding out who *she* was. Arbus called herself an explorer, and she was, no doubt, with all the requisite bravery and heedlessness. She was seeking the territory of the self.

But what she was also seeking, in all her shots, was the truth, what the secrets withheld. In diving into other people's secrets she dove into her own, in a sort of protected absentia. She was there and not there. The secrets were hers and not hers. It was a perfect arrangement, one of photography's special appeals. Arbus loved flaws. They were what got noticed first, before anything else, she figured. And what she kept seeing in these sex shots was, in a word, *ugliness*. Sex was a lot of things for her, but one thing it wasn't was pretty.

Yet another 1966 shot features a transvestite with a torn stocking. There's an illusion of cleavage. She wears a black negligee with garters. Her eyebrows are carefully drawn. She "passes," but angrily. Her look is accusatory. She's a woman, but hard, rough, homely. More than anything else she looks like she wants to beat someone up.

Arbus also shoots her on a couch. Again, as in the shot of the couple under a paper lantern, the walls are flophouse grimy. She stares blankly to the left of the camera with a look of disgust. Her hair is blonde but we see the dark roots, the reality beneath the contrivance.

A different shot from 1965 shows a couple on a couch (contact sheet number 4106). They are clothed this time. They both smoke. She appears drunk, heavy-lidded; he seems to be pushing her into something she does not want to do, several times putting her into a headlock. They flop down desultorily. There is something distastefully forceful about the man's intentions.

In 1968 Arbus captures a girl on her bed with her shirt off. She looks directly into the camera, her hair an afro, her breasts— the flaw—disarmingly tiny. It takes a moment or two to determine she's not in fact a man. The case seems far from clear. There's floral wallpaper behind her—it's unclean, as walls always are in these pictures. The sheets on her bed are disarranged. Her arms are thin, with long, diaphanous black hairs.

The book *Revelations* includes only one shot of a porn set, from 1968. It's brilliantly bizarre. The actors, male, kneel on a bed, hugging artificially, stiffly. In front of them sits a man with goatee, tie, and glasses, peering forlornly straight ahead in profile. It's a sad, silly, hopelessly furtive world on display. No spontaneity or enjoyment obtains.

The sex obsession commenced in earnest in 1965—following her father's death and Doon's departure for college—but it extended, too. For that reason it is difficult to date with any meaningful precision. It never really loosened its grip. In 1970, a year before her death, Arbus zooms in on a dominatrix with her client. How she gained access this time is a special marvel. The scene's grotesque. The woman's a blank in her bustier and black stocking, a breast poking out. She's performing a job—nothing more. The man looks infantile in his cloyingness. He wears glasses. He's middle-aged, flabby, clammy, in black socks. In another shot he kneels, the dominatrix behind him with a whip, legs spread. He's a sex junkie in thrall to his unsightly desires, ass raised for a spanking.

John Szarkowski, who curated the *New Documents* show of February 1967, references a large area of "private thought and feeling" in Arbus that he did not dare enter. Friendship with her he compares to a "masked ball," full of "elliptical codes." He calls her photography of mysteries so "shy, fugitive, and terrific that they [the mysteries], or she, might have been frightened off, had the issues been openly stated."[17]

For Arbus, it's true, photography was a secret about a secret. It was dirty, nasty, furtive. It was what she got away with, like

stealing cookies at night. With sex in the crosshairs, all these elements coalesced in flaw-filled unison. It's one more example of
the basically counterphobic nature of Arbus's art. In the same
way that she went into fear in order to be fearless, here she re-
pulses herself out of repulsion, shames shame. Few can say what
sort of pleasure Arbus got from sex, of whatever kind, in whatever setting. One thing's for certain, though. It never looks
good in her lens. The beds are soiled, the rooms are grimy and
dim, the bodies unappealing, the faces empty, angry, pinched.
Toward the end of her life Arbus planned a project on love. It's
what these shots never register. Still, she calls it dumb. She mentions sixty-year-old twins who dress alike, the lady with the
pet monkey, and a handicapped couple, one retarded, the other
three and a half feet tall with red hair. Angling in is another
prospect, the "local sado-masochistic community." There's a
man with a single phallic arm whom she meets. He's going to
inquire about Arbus shooting one of his parties. So love makes
its ephemeral appearance, then it's back to the seamy side.

One additional representation of this theme is Arbus's work on
nudists, which began before the sex adventures, in 1963. Nudism
isn't sex, exactly, but it speaks a similar language. Not according
to nudists, however, who told Arbus emphatically, "Sex is not a
problem in a nudist camp," a statement certain facts belie.

Arbus made a number of visits that she wrote about briefly.
One was to the Sunshine Camp in New Jersey in 1963, another
to Sunnyrest in 1965, in Pennsylvania. (The weather's good in
the land of nudity). She compared the experience to "walking
into a hallucination" not one's own.[18] The first person she sees
is a man mowing his lawn naked; others mill about comically

wearing nothing but a band-aid or a pencil behind their ears. The camp director goes out of his way to stress nudism's cleanliness. He calls it a "clean" way to live. He feels there is something clean about the human body, something intrinsic and pure that clothing elides. Overall, she's assured, "it's a good life," a "little like heaven."

Funnily, pictures on walls are mostly nudes, and magazines on coffee tables "largely girlie," Arbus notices. Peeping Toms can be a problem—boys from surrounding towns ogling from the woods, checking out the action. Grounds for eviction include a) staring or b) getting an erection. Still, according to camp visitors and officials, it's not the body itself that's obscene but the imagination. And at nudist camps, obscenity disappears because "nothing is left to the imagination."

In 1965 Arbus becomes an official "member of the movement," with all its associated privileges, including the license to travel around the nation and stay for a time in various camp settings. She plans "following where it leads in civilian life," meaning, apparently, how nudists live and function outside nudist enclaves.[19]

The shots that emerge are a mixed bag. There's a young, apron-wearing waitress, order pad tucked in a pocket, dirty feet in the sand. The look is self-consciously unself-conscious. Another young girl is fully nude, chubby around the middle, hair thrown to one side, posing in front of woods. There are families, too, some sprawling lazily on a lawn, and couples, in their rooms or out in the woods holding hands, as in the most famous shot of all, "A Husband and Wife in the Woods at a Nudist Camp, N.J. 1963." Here the woman's body dominates the scene, centered: She looks straight on. It almost becomes pure object, another tree, just whiter. She blends into nature. The man smiles. He appears to be holding in his right hand a pack of cigarettes. Nudists smoke too.

Arbus shot a lot of nudes—transvestites, strippers, random people in hotel rooms. So there's nothing particularly discontinuous about these pictures except their setting. And there's nothing discontinuous about Arbus's interest in the subject, her reactions to what she saw, her interpretation of nudism's deeper meanings. Both the shantytown visit as a child and the trips to circuses as an adult involved seeing things she was supposed to see but had never been allowed to, experiences denied her. She says the same about nudist camps, which she called "a terrific subject for me": She "always wanted to go but didn't dare tell anybody."[20] More naughtiness, in other words. More misbehavior.

And in an interpretation that comes as no surprise, one utterly expectable in light of her early history and core psychological attitude, Arbus reduces nudism to secrets. For nudists, she says, their presence in a camp is the "darkest secret of their lives," a fact unsuspected by friends and relatives, the "disclosure of which might bring disgrace." Her photography is dirty, a private sin; so is their nudism, its cleanness notwithstanding. She's aware of the disgracefulness of her work; their lifestyle elicits the same reaction.

Plus, what she finds isn't Edenic, but filthy. The glaringly white bodies fail to brighten up the surrounding forest. The lake "oozes mud" in a "particularly nasty" fashion. Empty pop bottles lie around. Rusty bobby pins scatter underfoot. The outhouse reeks, the woods—where she purposely poses her subjects—never fail to look "mangy." All told, it's as if "God allowed Adam and Eve to remain in the Garden of Eden," but they only got civilized, procreated, and mucked it up. Clothes or no clothes, the secret's there, and it mocks any counterinitiative. Nudists are just as dirty as nonnudists, maybe more so for pretending to be clean.

Camp was never a pleasant place for Arbus to be. It's where she risked secret telling of her own, with unhappy consequences. That nudists meet the same fate in her eyes makes obvious sense. Secrets, for Arbus, never get revealed upliftingly. They pounce, and it hurts.

In adolescence Arbus accepted the dares her wide-eyed friends declined, though she says she was actually more scared than anyone else. This was another of her secrets, the terror she worked to conceal. When it comes to sex, as an adult Arbus seldom alluded to any fear. She seems positively possessed—the objective, data-gathering participant-observer, immersed in the arcane rituals of misunderstood natives, emboldened by the camera's implicit license. If the fear's there, it's unexpressed, an emotional impediment sidestepped in the interest of science. Arbus sexualized everything, her psychotherapist Helen Boigon told me. Sex was the dominant theme of her therapy. And her behavior was compulsive. With the Kronhausens, for instance, it came unbidden. It surprised her, caught her off guard.

Compulsion is a form of *undoing*. It's a response to ego-dystonic thoughts—ideas at odds with the self. It's the price the thoughts exact; it's corrective. The thoughts are distasteful, alien; the behavior's a compensation.

Arbus's sex with complete strangers, deliberately sought, is a kind of self-punishment. She forced herself to do it as a means of exorcising feelings of shame, the clotted set of sins that never stopped agitating internally, bound up, most likely, with the so-called "sexual experimentation" tried with her brother Howard. Her desires rattled and raked her, photography was a greedy sin, and the sexual acting-out a move toward sinlessness, a debt she was trying to repay. Did she succeed? Maybe not. The price was high. And sexual preoccupations, once they began most forcefully in the mid-1960s, never got any less insistent. They remained active even in her final days.

So sex was a function of psychodynamics, a shame eraser in the best of cases, or simply a shame repeater, reenacted grimly and to no psychological benefit. But it also came straight out of Arbus's personality. Not that milieu wasn't an obvious factor. Being an artist in the 1960s, taking the kinds of shots she did in the kinds of places she frequented, no doubt threw her into situations where sex was atmospherically redolent. The opportunities would have been plentiful. It was a given. That Arbus succumbed from time to time is hardly surprising. She wasn't the only one to do so.

But there was also something unique about Arbus's appetites, something a lot more basic and fundamental at work. Her personality was configured in such a way as to make sex an emotional stabilizer. Sex was two things for her: a motive and a strategy.

There's a personality dimension Arbus was unusually high in, a so-called "artist type." It's called "openness to experience," and it's 57 percent heritable, according to research. To a degree, that is, Arbus was born with a basic endogenous tendency and its accompanying hard-wired motivational subcurrent. It made her seek out sensation wherever and whenever she could find it. In general terms, those high in "O" tend to be sensitive, passionate dreamers; they are curious, adventurous, easily bored; their emotional range is wider than average. They are freethinkers, unorthodox, prone to flouting convention.[21]

A portion of "O" has simply to do with how the mind is organized, how it's structured. There's a looseness to consciousness, a wider scope of awareness and a deeper and more intense pattern of engagement. High "O" people are less repressed, less defensive; they allow into consciousness impulses others might find unacceptable. High "O" also correlates with "regression in the service of the ego," another ability common to artists in general. Such people regress intentionally; they make easy, fluid contact with primitive modes of experience and behavior, then they use that material in their work. They go deeper into themselves, and—at least theoretically—resurface as necessary. They travel permeably between what some psychologists call primary and secondary process thinking—thinking that is at one extreme irrational, illogical, and intuitive, and at the other more conscious, controlled, and reality-oriented. They dive into psychic depths; they don't get yanked. They take the night journey on purpose, willfully.

This aspect of "O" fits Arbus perfectly. Her sense of reality was always emotionally and psychologically perfused. She speaks about her private sense of what a fact is and feels disoriented when others' "facts" don't match the facts as she envisions them. Her sense of the world was tied closely to her mental life.

She also made less-than-average use of repression. The range of feeling she accessed was wide. There was depression, of course—a state that correlates, according to research, with two facets of openness, feelings and aesthetics—but there was also rage, hate, anger, anxiety, love, empathy, excitement, joy. Her habit was not to block out feelings—as those high in defensiveness typically will—but to let them in. In the same vein, she had ready access to domains of experience ordinarily disavowed. The darkness rarely repelled her. She found it when she needed to, and it made frequent appearances in her subjectively driven pictures displaying what she registered internally. She found freaks outside but she found them inside too. She wasn't a flincher.

It's not clear, however, that Arbus's regression was ego-governed—self-controlled, intentional. She can seem, at times, fixated to trauma, cuing it up, replaying it self-defeatingly. There's a stuckness, a compulsiveness about her attraction to subterranean webs of association. They controlled her; the choice was not hers. And they also controlled her art. Its strangeness, its off-putting effect was borrowed in a way that increased its power. But it rarely if ever allowed for a rising above, a sense of redemption or restitution or salutary self-discovery.

The motive behind high "O" is a need for experience. What Arbus was about, maybe more than anything else, was just that. Experience was a word she used frequently. It was what she was after, it was the source of her adventurousness, her explorer mentality. Those with openness tendencies crave variety, sentience, understanding. Their curiosity is active, on the make. They seek out the unfamiliar, self-altering encounters with others and the world. The static leaves them restless and bored. They live for what Robert Hughes called "the shock of the new." This being the case, it comes as no surprise that openness correlates with another personality-based dimension, Zuckerman's "sensation-seeking," or SS. SS consists of four elements: thrill and adventure seeking, disinhibition of impulses, boredom susceptibility, and experience seeking. It's clear Arbus was a first-class sensation seeker. What's interesting is that high "O" correlates most powerfully with the "experience seeking" facet of SS. Arbus sought all sorts of experiences—carnivals, freak shows, twin conventions—but the one that increasingly trumped all others was sex. The thrill and adventure of sex inflamed her. It was experience seeking of the first order. It was also a temporary anodyne for boredom, for depression (which is often experienced as emptiness), and it altered and enlarged the self. Those with relatively mild needs for experience don't latch on to sex as a solution. For them, a little adventure is more than enough. Arbus was in a completely different category. Experience was a motive, a drive, no average striving. Sex fit the bill ideally. It was the best form of self-expression, right up there with her art.

There are additional, more minor ways that high "O" accounts for features of Arbus's psychology, at least in part. Empathy, independent achievement, and flexibility all correlate with "O." Social presence, or interpersonal poise, is also related to openness, and it's a talent Arbus put to effective use when getting her subjects to show her what she needed in a shot, or simply agreeing to being shot in the first place.

But sex is the question here. And for Arbus, sex was an offshoot, a uniquely *powerful* offshoot, of a basic endogenous tendency toward openness and, more to the point, a need for adventure and experience. Sex was intrinsically motivational for Arbus. It expressed her like nothing else.

There is another more functional, more learned factor at work that, combined with openness, makes Arbus's need for sex even more understandable. A lot of psychological research zeros in on the connection between sex and attachment—of the avoidant or anxious type. In short, sex provides an arena in which to gratify attachment needs. It gets used *strategically*. It's physically pleasurable—for most people, most of the time—but just as important, it meets *emotional* demands. Those anxiously attached, like Arbus, develop higher levels of desire for contact, closeness, and reassurance. Sex does the trick. According to research, attachment anxiety predicts voluntary but unwanted sex and risky sex—both Arbus predilections. Conditions for sexual activation and attachment-related motives for sex also include these: wanting sex especially when feeling insecure; using sex to establish emotional closeness; and most of all, seeking sex to feel reassured. Sex is protective: It overcomes anger and other negative moods in a lover. It's also manipulative, eliciting caregiving in times of distress.[22]

So for Arbus, two powerful factors operated simultaneously. They reinforced each other. She sought sex to gather up experience, to feel alive, stimulated, vitalized, inspired. But she used it to fend off anxiety, too, especially when others came across as disinterested, aloof, unresponsive, or unavailable—when they signaled they might not attend to her needs. Sex with strangers had mostly to do with the first factor—experience seeking. Strangers weren't attachment figures; their emotional value was nil. But with genuine love objects, people Arbus counted on for succor, experience was secondary, relationship primary. Arbus maintained closeness, guaranteed availability, by drawing people in sexually. Sex cemented attachment, at least in the moment. But it became compulsive and needy. There was a desperation.

Depression's tangled up in all this, too. First of all, it correlates, a little unexpectedly, with openness. Or, more specifically, with two of the six facets of openness, "aesthetics" and "feelings." The latter finding is easy to figure. High "O" implies a wider range of feeling and more tolerance for all sorts of emotional states, positive or negative. Open people feel excitement and joy; they also feel fear and sadness. They don't shut feeling down. "Aesthetics" has mostly to do with love of beauty, art, and imagination. The correlation between this facet and depression is in fact *higher* than it is for feelings. No one has any solid idea why. For decades research has linked creativity with depression, along with suicide and alcohol abuse.[23] So creativity itself can be crazy-making, for numberless reasons. There's the burden of making art, the deep draw on the psyche. There's also the fact that the art never quite lives up to what the artist envisioned. Success is usually partial and the partiality is a downer. Arbus herself said a picture was always more or less than what she imagined. "You never know . . . What comes out is not what you put in."[24]

Another possibility is that people who are especially attuned to beauty and the arts might just be more sensitive in general, more affected by negative events and stimuli. Sensitivity leads to reactivity, less of an ability to tune out what's going on.

Whatever the case, openness implies sadness. So does anxious attachment, which correlates with every single one of the following: depression, vulnerability, anxiety, self-consciousness, anger-hostility, impulsiveness, and a relative lack of positive affect. We already know Arbus was depressed. That's no revelation. She felt it as physical, chemical. But there were psychological aspects, too, bound up with openness and attachment insecurity and a need to erase shame.

Chapter 5

THE BLACK KNOT

ARBUS MADE LISTS. Maybe more, in fact, than she made photographs. They are all over her notebooks, on scraps of paper, in grant applications, in letters to magazine editors. It's simple. She didn't want to lose a good thought. The lists made slipping glimpses tangible; they were mental roadmaps, to read. "Seance, gypsies, horse show, aquarium . . . woodpeckerholes, pseudoplaces, skeptics . . . baton twirlers, microcephalics, proms, ritual." Sometimes entire phrases or sentences appeared, her own or passages copied out from books: "to lie in order to not be believed," "every shock is a symbolic withdrawal of support," "cruelty is often some extreme of compliment."[1] Inspirations came in bunches. Arbus was an idea machine, her mind a never-ending rush hour. She needed money, so there was always that impetus. After the separation, and after the divorce as well, Allan sent what cash he could, but alone it did not suffice. Besides, it was always important to Diane that she demonstrate financial independence, despite the fact that, much like her father, she was never especially good with money.

According to Bosworth she carried it around in crunched wads, almost never stepping into a bank. Some of these ideas therefore became pitches she sent out haphazardly for work, with whatever magazines or editors expressed interest. Others, those that held more viable appeal, she explored on her own. Who ever knew which car might shoot the gap?

In the summer of 1970, exactly one year before her suicide, Arbus was busy keeping busy, scanning the files of the *Daily News* and other photo sources for samples of fixations. It was almost a scientific endeavor. All signature Arbus fixations found a place on the list: "accident, grief, pain, death of pet animals, murder victims, corruption, people hiding their faces, kidnapping, execution, suicides, before, during, after; riots, strikes, cyclones, flood, fire, dust storms, depression, breadlines, child abuse, closeted children, people dying of mysterious disease, photographers being shot."[2] It's a Freudian free association, a web of perverse preoccupations full of individual topics—like breadlines, depression, closeted children—that would have resonated deeply. "People hiding their faces" recalls the shot of the Westchester family on their lawn, the father covering his eyes. Even kidnapping, a seemingly alien occurrence, was something Arbus feared as a child and wrote about in her adolescent autobiography. The last item—"photographers being shot"— grabbed Arbus especially. To her it was the perfect image. Two kinds of shooters, one managing, totally implausibly, to capture and arrest the precise moment of violence. Arbus loved that. These were the topics that caught her eye, that registered subjectively because of her unique biography, the images she sometimes cut out and taped to a wall above her bed for inspiration—of a dark sort, the sort that always got her going. The world she saw and the pictures she surrounded herself with were archaeological records of despair, danger, trauma. Even in her own shots, the faces that looked back at her *were* her, isolated fragments of discarded features of self. They covertly emphasized a basic misery. It was only a matter of time before the darkness got a little too dark. In fact, it was *always* too dark. Dark was Arbus's default setting.

The mood problem and the "great sad artist" romance started early—and never did stop. You couldn't miss Diane's moods, her sister Renee said. They were plain even in childhood, as the adolescent autobiography makes perfectly clear. In the years before her suicide Arbus called Renee regularly for long, searching conversations, wondering how to stem the tide. She pursued the same subject with her mother, who had been through her own trial of black blood. Gertrude somehow stepped out of the darkness, at least partially; Diane never made it. She stepped in, she stayed.

"I seem to be undergoing some subtle subterranean revolution," she says on July 4, 1968. "Signs erupt that seem portentous." Her work of that time—on whores, criminals, returned runaways, sex clubs, New Jersey prisons—was proceeding, as it usually seemed to do, "oddly and obsessively."[3] She had moved, with Doon and Amy, from Charles Street to a duplex at the top of a brownstone—the lease at Charles Street had expired, and there was a threat of a rent increase.[4] The new place Arbus finds better than expected, with three small bedrooms and two baths. It was just blocks away from St. Mark's Place, whose underground contained a "whole bunch of new heroes."[5] She alludes to Eddie Carmel, the Jewish Giant, a subject she first worries may be "too exotic." She notices a sudden and obscure upsurge of feeling impossible to pin down. "I need a dam," she decides. She wants to do something, find work, not just feel elated. In the midst of this her mother, widowed since 1963, remarried. Her new husband, Arbus notes comically, resembles a dentist.

Then around mid-July 1968 the portentousness got very real. Arbus suddenly found it hard to walk up the stairs to her own apartment. She felt profound fatigue; there was nausea and recurrent stomachaches. Clearly some sort of disease process was commencing; something was seriously amiss. Doctors figured, at first, that her symptoms were psychosomatic—signs of depression and its sapping of energy, its anxiety elements, its hypochondriacal features—or else menopause or merely old age. Yet on July 18, 1968, she crawls into the hospital for tests. The trip turned into a three-week stay. Portions of the liver were excised. At first no answers emerged; no one knew what was going on. Arbus, cheerful nonetheless, or putting up a brave front, tells her daughter Amy, "Illness is terrific for taking you back to the beginning like bankruptcy." She fantasized a cleansing starting-over, a fresh departure. Then a diagnosis arrived: hepatitis. She could not move for a day and had to be fed by an aide who jammed food sideways into her mouth: "I was a 45 yr old infant and angry to boot." Feeling suddenly shy, consumed by the extraordinary and absorbing difference between sickness and health, she wonders, with a sense of genuine relief: *What if I am no longer a photographer?* It's a remarkable, unexpected thought. The fact that she can't take photographs she finds almost cheering, "terribly good for me." She had a doctor's excuse not to shoot, a prescribed vacation from the obsessive friction, the grind of producing images. Hepatitis was the dam she was looking for. It felt liberating: "I have learned to see that no state of being is intrinsic or autonomous." One's self, Arbus finds, is dispensable. She could toss it away if she chose to, just as the self-deleting freaks did. "I lost my curiosity," she adds, but this was okay for a time. When at last she leaves the hospital, she is told to eat red meat and to take mounds of vitamins. She expects to be even better than new in a few months, she tells Amy. In a state of some perplexity, she impulsively asks a friend: "Can you catch hepatitis from going to bed with a lot of people you don't know?"[6]

The illness stymied, Arbus begins to think of work again, her refuge, her curse, and also her moneymaker. It isn't easy. She dreads taking pictures, pretends "I am an imposter," but hoists her camera around her neck without even using it, grateful just to wear it. But the hepatitis—despite the revivifying philosophizing that accompanied it, the thoughts of leaving the self or even photography behind—left in its wake a residue of depression that proved to be adhesive and disabling.

By October Arbus is "literally scared" of getting depressed. She finds the condition insidiously, irritatingly chemical. "Energy just leaks out," she says. A few short months later, in early 1969, Allan Arbus leaves for California—to become an actor in earnest. (He later starred in shows such as M*A*S*H, where he played the psychiatrist Sidney, ministering to stressed-out, overworked doctors.) In June the two are officially, though amicably, divorced. Arbus minimized any ensuing emotional pain. She tried making the divorce's impact innocuous, its meaning inconsequential, but Allan's leaving was a blow. A colossally important attachment figure, always there, always responsive and loving and sympathetic, a person she could trust, was now frighteningly gone, on the other side of the country. With no one left to shore her up—at least not like Allan could—and with her native resources at a dangerously low ebb, Arbus took the advice of a friend—the *brother* of a friend, to be precise—and began, for the very first time, psychotherapy, of a kind that would have to be called, from an analytic or any other relatively mainstream perspective, unorthodox.

The doctor was Helen Boigon, one year Arbus's senior, an analyst with an affection for the theories of neo-Freudian Karen Horney, who focused on what she termed basic anxiety and its neurotic sequelae: moving away (isolating, avoiding others), moving toward (seeking others out for comfort, needing them too much), and moving against (reacting to others with defensive anger, pushing them away). Boigon practiced in Manhattan for sixty years and taught, without remuneration, at the Horney Institute. She was a skilled, seasoned practitioner, steady, solid, wise, and open to new ideas, unafraid of taking sessions (and clients) down irregular avenues. She was a bit of a pioneer, anything but doctrinaire. For these reasons and others too she was a good fit, a promising choice for Arbus.

Therapy typically begins with some sort of "initial complaint" or "presenting problem," in the clinical vernacular. Patients arrive with clear issues that become the therapy's target. These were weirdly lacking in Arbus's case, or at least not focused on. Arbus was depressed, to be sure. She was anxious, fatigued. Her energy had fled to places unknown. She was dealing with the loss of Allan, struggling to make ends meet. But according to Boigon, who was eighty-three at the time I interviewed her—yet astonishingly lucid—Arbus "did not say" what brought her to the sessions initially. She "just wanted to talk." She did not mention the hepatitis diagnosis at all, nor was there any reference to suicide—no need, even, for any sort of formal suicide assessment, a common practice nowadays, virtually obligatory. In Boigon's recollection Arbus "just said she was feeling bad." This general badness was never circumscribed.[7]

Another priority when therapy begins is mutual agreement on a direction—the therapy's goals. Yet here again, there was "no sense of a definite path to be followed," according to Boigon. Things progressed more or less organically, with little obvious structure from session to session. Horney's model of personality, with its anxiety nucleus and contingent neurotic strategies for coping—in particular the defense of "moving toward" people, using others as a means of calming fear and deriving reassurance—seems on its face directly applicable to Arbus's basic modus operandi. She fled into others. Sometimes through sex, sometimes through the closeness, the intimacy she demanded of her subjects. But Boigon felt no need to apply these concepts; she worked, at this time, largely atheoretically. "We just accepted the phenomena as they evolved. Not to be explained—that was Diane."

In fact, this attitude—no explaining—was something Arbus herself latched on to as far back as 1960. The notion that psychic events were caused, that motives produced actions lawfully, that "one does something BECAUSE of something," left her cold. She rejected the linearity of psychological life. This is an odd position to take generally—it's the erasure of life history—but more so in the context of therapy with a person trained analytically, as Boigon was. The question of why would have been paramount. The entire effort goes toward unearthing hidden motives. In classic Freudian terms, childhood is key; understanding continuities is essential. These are the aims of interpretation, the goal being to restore lost or repressed links between the present and the past, to read the present as a disguised representation of unresolved prior conflicts and habits of being. But Arbus resisted going there. She hated the very idea. And for good reason. What Arbus felt she learned in the hospital was that no state of being was intrinsic, no element of self indispensable. One was free to be anything at all, at any time. Freaks taught her the same lesson. They made themselves up; they multiplied identity. So continuity, those largely hidden whys bound up in family origin, set limits on expression. They were causal, determinative. Hating the whys, hating motivation, equaled self-liberation. It was an untethering. It was also defensive, fear-driven. Not knowing, dismissing the very concept of knowing, sidestepped necessary confrontations. If it got Arbus nowhere, if it left her where she already was, so be it. Boigon would have needed to wrestle this attitude away from Arbus in order to confront the opacity at the core of her being, the avowed meaninglessness of a past, a history, a family environment.

Yet Boigon let Arbus lead. There never was any raid on the inarticulate. And the reason why may have much to do with Boigon's own biography. She had experienced an epiphany of her own, not altogether different from Arbus's. She, too, it turns out, was happy sidestepping more mulish Freudian dogmas. For a number of years Boigon taught Freud at the American Institute of Psychoanalysis. She says she did her best to remain "objective," but gradually, over time, found herself rejecting "most of what he asserts." In the end she left the Institute, along with nineteen others, over a "political blow-up." Horney's book, *Neurosis and Personal Growth,* was a key influence, but even its importance declined, largely due to a massively traumatic personal circumstance that left Boigon questioning much of what she had assumed to be true about life and personality.

Boigon had been happily married to her husband, Melvin, also an MD, for over twenty years. They had two children together, Seth and Margot (Seth became a social worker, Margot an MD). On December 29, 1968, "Mel" collapsed; he died, by Boigon's account, at midnight on New Year's Day, 1969, just months before she began seeing Arbus. There had been a rupture of an aneurysm at the Circle of Willis, also called the Willis Polygon, a set of arteries supplying blood to the brain. The arrangement of these arteries creates confusing redundancies in cerebral circulation; in some cases the redundancies themselves lead to reduced cerebral perfusion. As her husband had been in fine shape otherwise, the hospital asked for his heart, kidneys, and cornea; Boigon "gave instant permission," a decision that made the front page of the *Times* and was "broadcast around the country." She granted an interview to a radio station during which she was asked, most delicately, about her decision. "That's what my husband would have wanted," she said, "and besides, the body is only a temporary house; the soul goes to the next dimension."

Not having pondered such ideas before and finding herself more than a little surprised by what "flew out of" her mouth, Boigon embarked on a spiritual journey leading to the following startling, explosive conclusions: "I see us as a body, mind, and spirit (or soul). I believe in reincarnation and [the idea] that each trip we make in body is to learn a lesson—of which we are oblivious. I believe in the God of Emerson and Einstein—'We are seated in the lap of a Vast Intelligence.' I also believe that there are entities in the next dimension who try to give us some kind of help at times. I believe in the efficacy of prayer if it's yearning from the heart—words from the lips are no real help.

"I believe that what we call 'self' is a complex of evolving processes and that everyone is unique, complex, and to a degree irrational. At the bottom of what can be witnessed in an individual is an aesthetic—TASTE—subject to change without notice."

These are fascinating, fluid ideas. It's not clear how fully articulated they became during the period Boigon worked with Arbus or, for that matter, how they may have influenced the course of the therapy. But in a letter to Allan Arbus written in January 1970, Arbus records a comment by Boigon that uncannily duplicates her own earlier rejection of psychological motivation. "Dr. B," according to Arbus, called the pursuit of the "why" pointless. It went nowhere. It was a distraction, a misdirection. It cancels the subject and the *now* out, Boigon declared, when the "whole point (this is a graceless paraphrase) is in the experience of the Way It Is which WHY seeks to evade."[8]

So *why* missed the point. No doubt Arbus was thrilled to hear her own thoughts translated back to her. And Boigon's terrific notion of "taste," a more or less *aesthetic* concept of self, with its element of irrationality and volatility, would have appealed to Arbus too. Boigon had become by this time a phenomenologist, devoted to description (not cause) and the structure of lived experience. Her outlook was a little like R.D. Laing's, a writer Arbus admired, someone she imagined working with. Freud and Horney were long gone. The "way it is" trumped originology, the rooting of the present in remote past circumstance. Boigon's husband Mel once had asked her, a little Freudianly, if "emotional difficulties might not block a person from using his [artistic] gifts." Maybe so, she replied, but the line of thought held little magic. (Arbus's reaction would have been the same.) For Boigon, the common denominator [for the artist] "is neither excellence nor talent alone, but the will to do the work, *irrespective of motive.*" In the "saga of the artist (good, bad, or indifferent), the gift is inseparable from a blind urge to pursue." And though "many artists have been terribly sick and miserable in living, many are quite average as human beings . . . Feeling this in my blood and my bone now, I cannot urge anyone to work in art any more than I could exhort one to have faith . . . You have to have the will, the urge, the appetite, or the insincerity to self in itself will cut out the very essence that makes craft, *art.*" By which Boigon meant "the evolution of a unique *vision,* a personal idiom, that transforms color, form, and space, or clay into commentary." So art itself was simply *will.* Motive played no role at all. The work was purely expressive, a product of blind urges, not a disguised, veiled eruption of unconscious content moved from formlessness into form.

It's shocking how unaverage the therapy was at its core. No presenting problem, no goals, no interpretation, no seeking of insight, no attempt to link up a subterranean, powerful past with a present way of being, and finally, no explicit or even implicit pursuit of the cloaked *why.* Most of the time Arbus mentioned her ex-husband Allan, her daughters, her brother, only "en passant," in Boigon's phrase. "She flatly refused to say anything about her family"—a terrifically extraordinary exploratory posture— "saying she was sick of talking about them." Arbus even "paid little attention" to Boigon's questioning—"mainly 'What more comes to you about that?'"—perhaps because, in Boigon's formulation, "she was clearly a very anxious and angry person and chronically depressed."

Boigon and Arbus were simpatico when it came to the intellectual, conceptual side of the therapy equation. The two women were serendipitously like-minded there, and Boigon chose to allow Arbus to declare some topics simply out of bounds. Her attitude was one of passivity, of watchfulness, of hovering attention that did not pounce. For that reason the therapy, unlike many therapy experiences in which one deliberately works through difficult psychological terrain, required little struggle. At the beginning of the process Arbus writes, "Dr. B threatens to make me work, I get mad"—suggesting resistance of a sort that typically calls for interpretation. One wonders what Arbus was after. She wanted relief, but she was unusually reluctant to face the facts that might have allowed her to overcome the conflicts unnerving her. "I still don't move," Arbus realizes. The process was frustratingly slow going, for reasons traceable, perhaps, to its simple unusualness.

There's an old truism about psychotherapy. After three sessions, if the therapist and client do not feel as if they *like* each other, substantial benefit becomes unlikely. Rapport and affinity are key ingredients; theory and technique come second at best. Then, to complicate things a bit more, the client needs to get the sense that the therapist likes *her* too. It's about communicating empathy, something all clinical programs emphasize and even try teaching—if you don't have it, *fake* it. Faking it can suffice.

Initially Arbus wasn't so sure what she believed. "I begin to guess Dr. B may be OK," she says, indicating, at the least, uncertainty. She is *beginning* to *guess*. Boigon was less ambivalent. On one hand she maintains, "I never found Diane anything like terrifyingly freakish"—a reference to the art, most likely—"just, to me, very different from all of my other patients so my interest was sustained." Not a lot of strong feeling, in other words, more a sense of intellectual curiosity. At the same time she explains, "I did not like Diane, but I did not *dislike* her, or I would have stopped seeing her." So Boigon managed what she imagined to be a more or less harmless neutrality, not rare in the therapy setting. With a fascinating metaphor that underscores an essential incommensurability between the two women's quality of experience, Boigon compares herself to an "anthropologist who sat for several years at the outskirts of the forest waiting to try to make contact with a tribe known to be in the forest but never previously contacted." The art, too, "I really do not understand," Boigon says. "Every piece I can recall fills me with faint sadness—it does not excite me or create longing. It feels to me to tell of the regrettable part of life experience." At some point Arbus gave her a copy of the twins picture—"two sad faced little girls (cut off at the knees)." Though not her cup of tea, Boigon obligingly put it up, and according to Arbus "told me several stories of the reactions of patients."

For Boigon, Arbus disappeared amidst a bewildering tribe never previously documented; she was a wild child; she made herself visible and knowable only infrequently—"en passant"— popping up here and there, waving and spiriting off. She was more mirage than anything else, a secret about a secret, just like the art. Boigon crouched on the fringe of the forest, waiting for deeper connection or else merely watching the native life. Yet Arbus "just talked," sending out desultory signals, mentally

meandering as if unaware of Boigon's presence. Her actual behavior, too, was nowhere near conventional, in some instances
downright bizarre. There would be no pliant, diffident sitting
or lying down and, as in the stereotypical Freudian model, free-
associating.

Boigon met patients in a twenty-three-by-thirteen-foot office
with her club chair and stool facing the door. To the left was a
desk table behind which sat a narrower table with single draw-
ers up against the wall. The couch stood at the wall opposite
her chair; at the other end of the room were the windows, and
a foot away a comfortable chair. "I mention all this," Boigon
told me, "because Diane (as she asked me to call her) rarely
used either couch or chair. She would sashay up and down the
space, at times look at the objects on the shelves on the wall opposite the couch, or work her way to the window and gaze out,
or appear to study the stuff on the table I used as a desk. She
would move from couch to chair or from [the] chair [alone] to
fling herself on the floor beside my stool on which I kept my
legs elevated because of poor venous return."

What's clear from all this is that Arbus was stirred up. She
literally could not sit still, the wild energy still swelling, still
overflowing. A few obvious interpretations include anxiety—
which Boigon believed was prominent—or, just as likely, a so-
called "agitated depression"—depression with a strong anxiety
subcomponent. (Depression, according to research, puts one at
high risk for anxiety, and anxiety puts one at even higher risk
for depression. The two conditions, superficially dissimilar, actually tend to be strongly correlated; it's rare to find one without the other.)

In January 1971, six months before her suicide, Arbus writes,

"I been jittery. Waking at 4 AM," the latter an indicator of terminal or delayed insomnia, common in serious depressive episodes. "I have so much to learn about how to live," she says. "What have I been doing lo these 47 years?" A few modest insights emerge, but they don't prove to be transfiguring. On January 11, 1971, Arbus begins to question the value of consciousness, which itself can reflect disease (as Nietzsche once declared). Before she had regarded unawareness as a "sort of sin." She imagines moving past this—the need to know, the need to explain. Too much thought is worse than too little. It gums up the works. It's a condition all its own, as destructive, potentially, as anything else out there. Besides, "it doesn't matter what you do . . . except to yourself. I am always answering to someone who isn't even asking." Who raised the questions? Her critics? Lovers? Internalized attachment figures? Her family, all mention of whom she generally disallowed?

In the midst of this quasi-détente, something important occurred to alter the cagey mood of things. Arbus described the event in exceptional detail. It was obviously upsetting, though per usual she tiptoed around any serious implications. Near the end of January 1971, Arbus records, in a letter to Allan, a "hilarious" and "ridiculous" fight with Boigon. Apparently the Saturday appointments were very early—eight thirty A.M. Arbus had asked for a time change, but Boigon could not accommodate her. As Arbus arrived, the door was locked—not unprecedented—so she rang, and Boigon's son, Seth, appeared. Arbus describes him as a funny fat boy around the age of ten. The two visited, had great fun, then Seth moved off somewhere. By this time it was nine A.M. Arbus guessed, a little implausibly, that Boigon might have been testing her to see if she'd "get mad," an imputation of less than salutary motives, a projection of Arbus's irritation with Boigon's lateness and the early hour of the sessions themselves. But minutes later Boigon appeared, in a state of partial dress—robe, nightgown, sans makeup. "Who let you in?" she demanded, then disappeared again. When she returned, she (the capitalization is Arbus's) "SCOLDS ME FOR NOT HAVING KNOCKED ON HER DOOR OR ASKED SETH TO MAKE SURE SHE KNEW I WAS THERE . . . as if her understandable oversleeping was a symptom of MY illness. I was so furious. I burst into tears. Couldn't make her understand. SHE NEVER APOLOGIZED." Boigon, Arbus says, reframed the misunderstanding in terms of "what it showed about me." "Everything is really fine though," she decides.[9]

It's impossible now to reconstruct Boigon's interpretation of the event; she passed away before I had a chance to speak with her about it. But with just Arbus's account, certain meanings seem obvious, especially in light of the attachment history already described. By not knocking on Boigon's door, not attending to her own interests—talking, instead, with Boigon's son—Arbus was resisting the work of therapy. She was avoiding. From Boigon's perspective Arbus should have asserted herself, should have demanded to be seen. This was her time, after all, and she was wasting it. Arbus figures things differently. It is Boigon who has disappointed. Boigon should have attended to *her*. Boigon should have treated her as someone *worthy of being seen*. The oversleeping was a rejection, an unresponsiveness, a failure to be available. It incited fury and tears, and it called for an apology that never came. Funnily, Arbus tells us that everything is really fine. Only it isn't. Or at least we don't buy the sentiment. The "all caps" emphasis is simply too adamant for everything to really be fine. Boigon's oversleeping, the fact that she had forgotten about Arbus, her failure to notice this, her question *Who let you in*, and her scolding of Arbus for not taking care of her own interests—all this resonated deeply. It was another iteration of the theme of Arbus's life: She was worthy of a certain amount of attention, but that attention was not getting paid. Boigon had become the sleeping mother, the woman who smoked and drank coffee in her bedroom, the unloving zombie. Therapy occasions reenactments; behavior is memory in action, a code calling for interpretation; it needs to be seen symbolically in proper life-history context. Here, then, is Arbus's nuclear drama retold. Reaching out, however ambivalently and fearfully; eliciting a far less than satisfactory response, essentially a repudiation of needs; confusion, perplexity, bewilderment, followed by fury and tears. Seemingly tiny, prosaic, marginal episodes sometimes say a lot. This is one such instance.

The fact is, aside from the serendipitous agreement the two women reached concerning the "way it is" and the misguidedness of why-type probing, Boigon and Arbus were plainly very different people. She may have consoled herself with notions of Vast Intelligences and next dimensions, but Boigon was first and foremost a scientist, an MD. Her tastes were epicurean. She was practical, firm, a bit withheld. Freaks fascinated her not one iota. In comparison, Arbus was the unwashed aborigine. She was chiefly a "dramatist"—Boigon's term—"not scientifically-minded at all." And the looseness of her mind, her intuitiveness, her apparent absence of repression, the eccentricities of her behavior—in short, the way her mind worked and organized itself—all these things brought about a basic temperamental disconnect. Arbus's openness, the trait that defined her as much as any other, clashed with Boigon's restraint. There was a misalignment of basic tendencies.

And in pivotal moments the disconnect deepened. Yet another incident, far more bizarre, introduced fresh dimensions of discord. In the midst of all the pacing, kneeling, "plunking down on the floor," as Boigon put it—the agitated refusal to simply sit still and work—Arbus once, and *just once* (Boigon's emphasis), tried caressing Boigon's legs "with a somewhat slimy expression on her face . . . she postured and grimaced frequently." This is the sort of thing therapists dread. Dealing effectively with moments like these is a part of their training. Boigon, to her credit, was crystal clear, measured, self-possessed: "I told her she could say whatever she pleased, but she could not under any circumstances touch my person . . . I felt it as a coming-on to me. I said, 'I don't like that.'" Boigon, in other words, insisted on and reestablished boundaries. She set a limit. A bit like a parent, she said no. Boigon never described Arbus's reaction. But there would be no repeat, no future "slimy" overtures, so the message registered. Arbus apparently understood there were things she could not do.

Still, this was vintage Arbus. It's yet another example of how she used sex as a way of pushing her needs forward, of making people react to her, see her, *love* her. That she tried this sort of sexual game with her therapist, in a setting so utterly unlikely, so antithetical, only underscores the behavior's automatic, overlearned aspects. Average closeness was not enough for Arbus. The void was too capacious. People needed to be *entirely* available, *entirely* responsive—so sex tested their willingness and proved their commitment, their sensitivity to her misery. These two incidents—the appointment snafu and the ill-conceived seduction—pivot around Arbus's attachment insecurity, like so much of what she did. They dramatize insecurity's effects perfectly. Arbus arrives right on time, just as she's supposed to, but no one is there: The object is unavailable. It is the microcosmic story of Arbus's early life. Then, to make matters worse, she's scolded, rejected. The therapist/mother disappoints again. Then, in the case of the seduction, she's being listened to, she's being heard, but the response is insufficient, it's somehow not enough, so she tries deepening it, activates a strategy—sex—that's evolved over a number of years and that's usually worked. But this time it misfires—another repudiation.

Although it wasn't ever interpreted (in keeping with the therapy's descriptive mode) or placed in any sort of biographical, emotional context—an effort that would have clarified its psychological function—sex was a key theme throughout the sessions. In fact, it was the main thing on Arbus's mind. It was what she wanted to talk about more than anything else. Boigon's feeling was that Arbus "sexualized everything." Sex was the atmosphere within which life moved. It was the fuel injection Arbus needed to feel. Not even art stood apart; it also rotated around sex's axis.

The photographer Stephen Frank recalls an Arbus lecture at the Rhode Island School of Design. This was 1970, in the midst of Arbus's therapy, so there's temporal contiguity. The students were enthralled. There was the work she showed, images not so recognizable then, not yet iconic—the newness and freshness of them, the audacity of the freaks' confederacy. But there was also Diane. Her person resonated more than the shots. "She was very sexy," Frank recalls. "She told stories about her photographs, and she had a great sexual anecdote for every picture, and by the time she was finished we were all in love with her. You just felt like you could tell her whatever your sexual fantasy was, and she would understand—there were no taboos."[10]

Taboos, of course, never meant much to Arbus. She scorched them with gusto—in her life and her art. She blew them up. This was *openness* at work, a craving for experience, but it was also neurotic, a compulsion. One thing that came up often during therapy was Arbus's sexual acting out. She took delight in cataloguing her "sexual exploits with total strangers who struck her as bizarre in their appearance," people she made twisted efforts to seduce. She wasn't always successful, Boigon says, but not for lack of trying. "She was doing all sorts of such things," Boigon explains, and if freaks were a terrible obsession, she was, Boigon emphasizes, "just as much obsessed by sex." Arbus never could name what was going on, never could provide any glittering rationale, any deep purpose. She was looking for "experience," Boigon concludes. "That's all she could name it."

There was more experience seeking than just this, more taboo thrashing. A major theme of the therapy was Marvin Israel—an innovative art director and graphic designer and Arbus's chief collaborator (Richard Avedon's too), whom she met in 1959, on the heels of his work as art director for *Seventeen* magazine, and whose importance in her life skyrocketed with Allan's departure to California. For a time they wrote to each other nearly every day, both struck by the various ways their lives intersected: "parents in the women's clothing business, an Ethical Culture education."[11] Israel, who died in 1984, also painted, though his talents in that medium have gone largely unappreciated. One show from the mid-1970s featured black-paletted dogs, "fiercely antagonistic, wolflike creatures that savagely bite, claw, and otherwise attack one another." Others, like a trio in *Untitled (Three Dogs in a Corner),* look locked in three-way sex, according to Grace Glueck in a *New York Times* review. Israel apparently loved animals and even called his own dog Marvin, a fact supporting his confession that the paintings were meta-phorical self-portraits. Another piece, *Hanging Dog,* sketches what Leffingwell in *Art in America* calls a "bizarre scenario for suicide or an act of erotic asphyxiation." As Glueck concludes, the work packs a "real wallop." It's certainly in the Arbus zone for its off-puttingness, its repugnance and viciousness. Like Arbus's work, it's very "not-nice."

Israel didn't just help Arbus plan projects or sift through her images with her, selecting best shots, or push her, as he did with other artists, in the direction of her obsessions and perversions. He was also her lover, and in the months preceding her suicide the object of great fury—again, I think, rooted in attachment insecurity. Boigon says the married Israel was a sex-games part-ner for Arbus. In fact, she "counted on him" to create scenarios that, in one guise, included the manufacture of various kinds of dildos, of the sort the Kronhausens collected. But he began to refuse, Boigon says. "He was slacking off," failing to provide the accustomed "sexual stimulus." And that put Arbus in a real state. The rage was ongoing, and it dominated therapy.

It's hard to say for sure, but according to Boigon it was Arbus's needs pushing the relationship, not Israel's. The sex games were about her. Israel complied for a time, possibly reluctantly, but it all became too much, Arbus's demands too intense, too insis-tent. She always wanted to go *beyond.* Enough never quite cut it. She "made no secret," says Elisabeth Sussman, "of the fact that she was waiting and waiting for Marvin's attention." So when Israel begged off, Arbus went into red alert. Here was another emotional refusal, another absence of faith. These moments Arbus never could abide. It goes back to the adolescent autobiography. She dropped the secret and it backfired. The closeness was curtailed, dialed back. So Arbus amped the system up. She went into hyperactivating mode. Israel became an obsession. And as he stopped giving back, the obsession predictably intensified. It was axiomatic. It was a turbulent stasis Boigon kept having to navigate. Per usual, she didn't interpret. She just listened to Arbus vent and rail. She watched the rage.

Israel's work in the mid-1970s, four years or so after Arbus's suicide, references what went on between the two of them. The attacking creatures biting and clawing, the three-way sex, the disturbed suicide scenario—it's one macabre motif after another. It's true, Israel did finally scale back his involvement with Arbus. But for a time he must have been ready and willing, and it's likely the games went far beyond dildos, if the art is any indication. Probably because of guilt—about Israel's wife, Margie Ponce Israel—or the nature of the sex games themselves, Arbus didn't discuss Israel with friends, just as she tended not to discuss her brother, Howard. And when the two took a trip to Germany together in February 1971, Arbus was ambivalent. "Nearly have cold feet," she says. And "to Germany. gulp. feel all jittery."[12]

Artist Mary Frank knew Israel and Arbus independently. "Marvin," she says, "could not have given Diane that feeling [of being cared for]. He was a very complicated person, and interested in his own powers." Though capable of kindness on occasion, "there was always this explosive aspect," Frank recalls.

And when Frank saw Arbus despondent, "it definitely had to do with Marvin." Boigon's feeling was the same. Israel was making Arbus miserable. And the misery showed no signs of abating. It mounted.

Israel wasn't Arbus's only sex-games partner, of course. We've already seen the degree to which sex came to dominate her life, and her art, in the years preceding her suicide. It was a magic solution, depression's elixir, a compulsion like any other. Arbus's brother, Howard Nemerov, touched on the sexual experimentation the two tried out as kids. That episode came up in therapy too. According to Boigon, Arbus described her brother as one of her more intriguing sexual playmates. Arbus seemed, Boigon believed, to be referring to more than just childhood games. The suggestion was that she and her brother had sex. But there was no elaboration, and Boigon never pushed it. The possibility remained, forever, yet another of Arbus's long-thought-out secrets. As even Allan Arbus said recently, "I never thought that I knew all her secrets," though she probably knew his.

Boigon's sense of the therapy's progress was always uncertain. "I assumed our sessions gave her something although I knew not what." Arbus was always on time, Boigon notes, and she expressed regret whenever she had to miss a session because of a job, what she did for magazines to make money, work that became another source of anger for her.

Some of the difficulty Boigon felt in putting her finger on the worth of the sessions, their meaning and direction, how Arbus felt about them, may have had to do with Arbus herself, whom Boigon formulated as "one of those rare schizoid personalities who manage to make a place for themselves in society and can be very interesting if one manages to get beyond the peculiar *persona*."

It was depression and anxiety, its close cousin, that brought Arbus into therapy in the first place. But those are episodic states. They fluctuate; in the best of cases, they remit. *Schizoid,* on the other hand, denotes an inflexible, unremitting organization of personality. Lisette Model, too, called Arbus schizophrenic, but she also called her neurotic, an utterly different form of pathology. But Model was no psychotherapist, no expert; Boigon was.

And hearing Arbus speak, what comes through immediately is the loose and tangential nature of her thought. She was all over the map. One waits in vain for any clear linearity. Theorists like Ronald Fairbairn, whose work Boigon would have been familiar with, describe four main "schizoid" themes: a concern with interpersonal distance; the use of self-preservative defenses that often take the form of exaggerated self-reliance; tension between anxiety-perfused needs to attach and antithetical demands for distance; and an overvaluation of the inner world at the expense of the outer. These themes do describe Arbus, especially the latter two. Attachment was the core conflict of her life; one sees its effects on her everywhere. Even from adolescence, she wanted to be intensely close, but she feared closeness, too; it let her down, unglued her. And if Boigon is certain about anything, it's the degree to which Arbus privileged her interior. Reality was nothing to her. It didn't register at all. Secrets, obsessions, sex, perversion, fantasy—these were Arbus's bread and butter. The world fell off into inconsequentiality.

Organized psychiatry's *Diagnostic and Statistical Manual of Mental Disorders*, the DSM for short, a deeply problematic taxonomy of questionable validity and spotty reliability, includes its own "schizoid" syndrome. It's a so-called Cluster C disorder—the odd and eccentric cluster—along with schizotypal, paranoid, and avoidant personality. As usual, it's not the least bit dynamic, not at all Fairbairnian. Detachment is a key ingredient (per the DSM). Other components include emotional coldness and "flatness," indifference to praise or criticism, the absence of friends, a preference for solitary activities, and zero interest in sexual activities. Clearly, using the DSM as a field guide, Arbus isn't even in the schizoid ballpark. She's as un-schizoid as one can be.

I don't think it matters much what Arbus *was*. Labels don't advance understanding. It's easy enough to throw names at anyone, anywhere. That's what a lot of psychiatry passes for nowadays, the hurling of diagnostic darts, every toss a bull's-eye. But I do think Boigon fell victim to a conflation—between schizoid phenomena and openness. Arbus was odd and eccentric, no doubt, but she was too good with people to be schizoid. She wasn't an extravert, but she worked her subjects cannily, draining them of secrets and shooting the effects. Her thinking was supple, divergent, original, odd, chaotic, irrational, intuitive. In a word, *creative*. What's clear is that Arbus struck Boigon as, simply, weird. She wasn't like any of her other patients, Boigon said. So "schizoid" quickly summed up an impression of apartness Boigon felt. But the real, more valid difference was that Arbus was an artist—she thought like an artist, she even wrote like an artist, in the shockingly accomplished, inventive texts accompanying a number of her magazine spreads. Openness includes magical ideation, perceptual aberration, primary-process thinking (illogical, contradictory, disorganized, unconsciously directed). This is the stuff Boigon noticed; this was the aspect of personality she homed in on. "Schizoid" was a rough, more pathological estimate. Arbus had her pathologies, but alongside them, predating them, was a basic endogenous tendency dictating creative thought from the very beginning. Her grade-school teachers were right—she *was* an artist. And though she doubted the idea at first, doing so over the long haul would have required nothing less than self-cancellation.

In light of its Zenlike aimlessness, it's hard to assess the therapy's effectiveness. There were no goals, and therefore no outcomes to judge. But the depression lingered and worsened. So did the rage, its target—Israel—unresponsive. Rage is tricky psychologically. It's restive; it has a way of finding objects, even blameless ones, unsuitable ones. But inevitably, unless it exhausts itself, burns up its own fuel, it returns to the source—the self from which it originated. It takes the self as an object after other options fade. Arbus never indicated anything leading Boigon to suspect suicide. The subject wasn't broached; Boigon saw no need to raise it. So there were two miscalculations—Boigon's and Arbus's. Because as Boigon told me—and on this subject she was emphatic, whether defensively or not—Arbus did not mean to die. Boigon never saw it coming, and if she's correct, neither did Arbus.

Chapter 6

SWEEPING BACK THE OCEAN

J UST PRIOR TO reproducing the results of Diane Arbus's
autopsy—along with a scan from the original document on
a facing page—the Arbus book *Revelations* offers this succinct
analysis of her suicide: "[It was] neither inevitable nor spontaneous, neither perplexing nor intelligible."[1] That's an interesting
take, on a lot of different levels. It's true, we never know exactly
why healthy people kill themselves, just as we never know exactly why people make the art they make. Answers don't come
easy if they come at all. There is always going to be, about everything, a fraction of unintelligibility. And when it comes right
down to it, maybe we don't want to know. As the philosopher
Ludwig Wittgenstein, himself no stranger to suicidal thinking
and impulses, said: If suicide is possible, then everything is possible. Suicide nullifies values. It is a rejection of purpose. It is
a threat to all those things that allow us to go on, to continue
living. Another philosopher, Camus, found suicide an incredibly arresting subject too. His ethics actually began with the

question "Why not kill yourself?" as a starting point for all inquiry into the meaning and motive for life.

The stymied response that accompanies suicides, that catch-22 of both wanting to know and not wanting to know, or knowing and not knowing, is proposed by the Arbus estate as the only possible or permissible last judgment. What she did isn't perplexing but it also isn't understandable. The slightly (but only slightly) subtler message is, Don't go there. Stay away. Her suicide was the outcome of some sort of process, but the process was not inevitable, nor was what she did spontaneous or relatively uncaused. She can be known, but she can't be known. We're left with a koan.

What do I think? Just as I find Arbus to be perplexing—as anyone looked at closely enough tends to be perplexing—I find her suicide perplexing too, but not unintelligible. Fundamentally suicide is a behavior, an act, like falling in love is an act, like taking pictures is an act. For someone wanting to understand it, it comes with an extra atmosphere of foreboding, sadness, and ambivalence, but suicide *in principle* is no less understandable than any of the other things people do. Reasons can be adduced. Some can be shown to be more compelling than others. And while the individual instance will always, to varying degrees, defy the soulless formulae invented to make sense of the act, that doesn't mean we come up empty-handed. Incrementally the interpreter produces a picture, advances toward ever-diminishing states of doubt. If the final product is a little blurry, it is not the case that we see nothing. This chapter, then—in fact, this book as a whole—aims for the blurry picture. But that's what people are. Personality is blurry. Life itself is blurry. We live in ambiguity. We die there too.

Suicide introduces additional entanglements, too, beyond the question of knowing or even wanting to know in the first place. For one, it can artificially prefigure analyses of any life in which it occurs. In other words, it casts a very heavy pall. It hovers there darkly in the background, that final act, and the impulse that really ought to be fought against is to search a bit too avidly for precursors, for the obscurist hints or omens. In the worst of cases, everything about the person gets read backward according to a suicide terminus. The story's end transforms conclusions about its beginnings and middles. I hope to avoid that here. I don't think *everything* about Arbus has to be subsumed under the fact of her suicide. Lots of the things she did obviously have nothing to do with how she ended her life. At the same time, I want to try understanding her death. The topic can hardly be avoided. So I discuss *some* of those elements of her psychology that amount, when assembled together, to a *sum of reasons*.

Artist suicide is another possible entanglement. The temptation is to suggest some kind of relation between the act and the art. We look in the art for a secret, dark calculus. But are these correlations real or illusory? Take, for instance, the case of Sylvia Plath, probably the most intensely researched suicide of all, maybe next to Hemingway. In the weeks leading up to her death she was writing what many consider to be her best work. It was dark, searing, eerie, and bold; it seemed to come to her relentlessly. She had broken through. She went down very deep, the imagery was sometimes virtually psychotic, and she never found a way out. One could say the poems, many on the subject of suicide, killed her. She paid the price for her genius. It cost her her life. At least that's how it seems.

There is van Gogh too, his last paintings of crows and wheat fields. In one that was possibly still on his easel when he shot himself in the stomach, three roads can be seen. The perspective is confusingly reversed. The roads do not converge at a horizon line, as they should. They *diverge*, pointing back at van Gogh himself, or "racing menacingly towards the painter-spectator," Heiman, a psychoanalyst, writes. "The vanishing point is the point of death." This is the painting of a man who, moreover, "cannot bear to continue life any longer. He has reached the end of his voyage through life. Death has come to claim his life: to claim it aggressively, murderously."[2] The crows, too, as symbols of death, "approach us menacingly as if attacking us." Heiman calls the work a "suicide painting." The message, he says, is not of a person ready to surrender himself to death—like, say, through drowning—but of "someone who is confronted with and afraid of being attacked, killed—and possibly devoured."

Kurt Cobain is a more recent case. While just starting out as a musician, even before the band Nirvana was formed, he apparently spoke of a wish to die young, thereby assuring his lasting fame as a rock-star icon, like Jim Morrison or Janis Joplin or another artist less known but more talented, Elliott Smith. As a child he made a kind of home video titled *Kurt Cobain Commits Bloody Suicide*. (There had been a suicide in the family; his grandfather's brother shot himself.) One album, his last (*In Utero*), he initially intended to title *I Hate Myself and Want to Die*. Individual songs make frequent reference to guns—for instance the painfully ironic line "I swear I don't have a gun" that he repeats throughout the tune "Come as You Are." (Cobain shot himself with a shotgun after taking what some consider a lethal dose of heroin.) The lyrics to the song are opaque and interesting. In it he seems to be addressing a person, a "friend" and "enemy" combined whom he tells "don't delay." It's possible this friend, or enemy, is death. He wants it to take its time but to hurry up as well. In one of his later songs he refers to the feeling of being "locked inside a heart-shaped box," a sort of coffin of love, and also being "drawn into a magnet," a "tarpit trap." In his suicide note, death is represented as preferable to living a life he considers false. Fame kills him. The rock-star role was a persona he was temperamentally unsuited for, just like the shy Jim Morrison and the self-doubting Elvis Presley.

Artists who suicide—the list is long and illustrious. Books have been written on the subject, none especially satisfying. Arbus's death can be looked at in ways similar to Plath's, van Gogh's, and Cobain's. There are congruities, however slight, however partial. Like Plath, Arbus in the period preceding her suicide felt as if she was taking the pictures she was always after but never quite getting before. That is, she was doing her best work—this being the photos of the mentally retarded, many shot in institutions around Halloween. Like van Gogh and the wheat fields, in which perspective seems to be reversed entirely, these pictures simply look odd. The light is crepuscular; they exist in a chaotic nowhereland, a combination dream and fairy tale. Doon Arbus in her afterword to the work sees it as a clear departure, a new direction. And like Cobain, she chose the simultaneous use of two suicide methods—Arbus slit her wrists but also took an overdose, as if wanting to make sure she did not last out the attempt. She was, also like Cobain—like Plath and van Gogh too, in fact—mired in relationship difficulties, these concerning her lover and mentor Marvin Israel.

So the questions are many. Some, such as A. Alvarez, Plath's good friend and fellow poet, have argued that Plath did not intend to die, that she expected to be found by an au pair girl who was due to arrive early on the morning of Plath's death. The same possibility exists for Arbus. Did she mean to die, or was she trying to punish someone by harming herself so severely, as Boigon contends? In a different vein, is there some connection between Arbus's last pictures and her suicide? Did the work she was doing hasten her demise, worsen her depression, or was it a nonfactor, incidental to the act? These are a few of the mysteries this chapter, and the chapter to follow, takes up, not so much to solve them but to introduce and examine a few hypotheses.

But let's begin with the facts, the biography, those features of Arbus's psychology and life history that urged her along a very dark arc, one that seems to have begun with her attraction to the idea of becoming, somehow, in some way, a great sad artist, and using her art to get certain difficult feelings and perceptions out, in the hope of, as Kafka put it, closing her eyes on them.

We know that Arbus's mother was depressed and maybe even suicidal when Diane was in her early teens—if not earlier— right around the time Arbus wrote her second autobiography. The two didn't discuss Gertrude's condition until much later, although Gertrude felt Diane was obliquely aware of what she was going through. Research shows that the offspring of depressed parents are at increased risk for depression. Specifically, 40 to 60 percent of preteen girls with depressed mothers develop a depressive disorder before they reach adulthood. Studies also indicate increased depression in *both* sons and daughters but only in relation to *maternal*, not paternal, depression. Daughters of depressed mothers have been shown to be at higher risk for anxiety as well, a finding underscoring a large volume of research revealing high comorbidity between anxiety and depression.[3] So, whether because of biological or psychological factors, depression was a relatively likely outcome for Diane—anxiety too. Making matters worse, her attachment insecurity also puts her at higher risk. Those with a history of suicidal behavior tend to have what researchers call a preoccupied attachment style—that is, like Arbus, they fear rejection and focus excessively on attachment relationships and trauma, with intermittent displays of anger and helplessness.[4] Arbus's adolescent autobiography fits this description perfectly. She's obsessed with relationships, with the question of trust, but they always disappoint her; she never gets what she wants out of them. Her ambivalence is acute; she can't love without fear. She's angry a lot of the time, and she feels like there's little she can do about it.

It was obviously a heavy atmosphere. And from the moment her talents were recognized, a bit too avidly for Arbus's tastes—her mistrust extending to her teachers' judgments about her work—it wasn't only art she finally, ambivalently foreclosed on. There was that hovering adjective. Great art, yes. But great *sad* art. For Arbus there didn't seem to be any other kind. The art began when the depression did. The two were therefore automatically aligned. All art, in fact most everything we do, is affect-driven. We are constantly scripting, narrating, interpreting, organizing, and sometimes, when possible, reversing feelings. The feelings Arbus dealt with were difficult from day one. The art's function was to interpret them, organize them, disclose them, and also to find them in others, whether there or not.

But most of the time the art wasn't quite enough. It just restated the sadness. In the wake of her *New Documents* show in March 1967 at the Museum of Modern Art, as a result of which she received a large amount of critical attention for the first time, and which some have called "the high point of Diane's life," Arbus lapsed into another depression. She didn't enjoy the attention, although at first, according to photographer Garry Winogrand, whose work was also on display, "she thought it was the greatest thing that had ever happened."[5] A friend, Tina Fredericks, says Arbus complained about feeling dry and flat. She said nobody understood her pictures. She felt her motives were being misread. Her art *was* her. And if she wished to be known somehow, to confess secrets, then the work failed her. In the eye of the public, she was nothing but a sick, weird voyeur, obsessed with freaks.

Around the same time, in the summer of 1967, Arbus was still seriously into the sexual self-exploration that began in 1965. She told the editor of the London *Sunday Times* about the orgies she'd been attending, and how after separating from Allan she had begun "having sex with as many people as possible, partially to test herself." The quickest, purest way to puncture a person's facade, she believed, was "through fucking." She was searching "for an authenticity of experience."[6] There was a random encounter with a sailor in the back of a Greyhound bus, the seduction of a powerful Washington lawyer, the picking up of a Puerto Rican boy on Third Avenue—a wide array of what she called "adventures." The editor to whom all this was confided, Peter Crookston, also had sex with Arbus, who apparently asked him afterward, "What are you doing with me? I go to bed with old men, young boys . . ."[7] Some, such as Marvin Israel, doubt such tales, calling them exaggerated and curiously improbable. On the other hand, they seem perfectly consistent with other facts about Arbus's sexual appetites, such as those recounted by the Kronhausens and Helen Boigon. An odd detail underscoring her sexual preoccupations, reported by several acquaintances, is an interest in showing around a sheaf of photos featuring genitalia, which she called some of the best pictures she'd ever seen. Later, in 1970, a student in Arbus's master photography class at Westbeth, who came to her rooms in order to take her portrait, recalls seeing tacked up on a wall pictures of penises—anatomical studies, none taken by Arbus—emerging out of navels.[8]

On occasion Arbus did manage to photograph group-sex parties (this was 1968). She had taken to following around a Reichian therapy aficionado named Stanley Fisher.[9] Reich believed that orgasm was the key to a happy, healthy life. But Neil Selkirk, who printed most of Arbus's work after her death, knows of only two erotic pictures in her files, one of a couple having bizarrely detached sex, another of a bondage house. "She did photograph at some orgies," Selkirk says, "but obviously she didn't think that the results were impressive enough to keep."[10]

In June 1968 Arbus and her daughters moved to a duplex at the top of a brownstone. Her landlady, hoping to make her happy and more comfortable in the new residence, bought her a white refrigerator. "I got the feeling she was depressed and anxious," the landlady said. "I got that feeling every time I saw her."[11] Arbus was now on an antidepressant, Vivactil—a decision Boigon took exception to—but she was weak and losing weight. Vivactil is a so-called tricyclic, so named because of its three-part chemical structure. It's theorized to work by blocking the reuptake of serotonin and norepinephrine. It increases anxiety and agitation in some people, and it can worsen symptoms of mania and schizophrenia. Now, too, we know that antidepressants occasionally increase suicidal thinking and behavior, a subject I'll return to later.

A doctor Arbus saw diagnosed her as anemic. She was prescribed a high-protein diet.

By July 1968 Arbus had lost eight pounds and was dogged by a fatigue that seemed to be intensifying slowly over time. Tests revealed the toxic hepatitis described before, "ostensibly secondary to the combination of drugs used for depression [Vivactil] and birth control."[12] She was taken off all medicines and started on a vitamin regimen. She returned home to recuperate, but noticed during her convalescence a "strange rage" . . . that came nightly. Its "werewolf" like visits left her reeling. It felt like a raw wild power. "I don't know how you make it energy."[13]

The rage—possibly part perimenopausal in origin, or connected with the stopping of the birth-control medicines—is a little surprising. But as we saw already, Arbus's hospital stay and her recuperation prevented the shooting of pictures. At first she enjoyed the vacation from artmaking, from the compulsive need to photograph. The anger was part impatience—a wish to get back to what made her feel most alive—and part residue, of deeper feelings that found outlets in the art. Since the art wasn't happening, the rage had nowhere to go. It just stayed home, so to speak, and Arbus was made to face it rather than displacing it, her more common strategy.

She relates the following dream, an encapsulation of a number of conflicts centered on the pursuit of lovers unresponsive and unavailable: "I dreamed that Rene d'Harnoncourt was my doctor [d'Harnoncourt was an art curator who, like Arbus, came from a wealthy family] . . . He was 9 ft tall. I could never reach him." This detail brings to mind Eddie Carmel, "the Jewish

Giant" Arbus took pictures of over the span of several years. As the dream continues she confronts this colossus, demanding that he explain the source of her ills. She wants an answer, she wants a remedy. But he scurries off, pretending not to hear, "looking elated like a mad scientist who has discovered a cure that kills people." At last he shape-shifts, reduces himself to shadow, then splits "into lots of silhouetted little men scurrying off in different directions so there was no way of knowing whom to pursue and I realized you are dead when you ask the doctor why you are sick and he doesn't hear you."[14]

A question concerns how Arbus may have contracted the hepatitis. People at risk include workers in the health professions, intravenous drug users, and hemophiliacs. Arbus was none of these. But she does fall into another high-risk category: those with multiple sexual partners. Her promiscuity may have made her sick, a possibility she had actually entertained and asked about.

Stuck in depression, irritable, prone to sudden tearfulness, Arbus was described by a visitor, Bill Jay (a photography teacher and writer), as "very energetic, and I guessed she could be extremely explosive—hot-tempered, even. She didn't smile or observe the usual pleasantries."[15] Although, after serving Jay a bizarre, foul-tasting concoction of cold jelly, she did warm up some. Others saw her as giggly, or they were struck by an aura of aloneness about her. Gail Sheehy, with whom she worked on a story for *New York* magazine, recalls her interest in the question of how one coped with loneliness. It was at this time that Studs Terkel interviewed Arbus for the book he was working on about the Great Depression of the 1930s. She "looked like a little girl to me," he said. "She wasn't quite there. Even though she was warm and friendly and terribly vulnerable, she was never quite there. And she had so little self-esteem. So many self-doubts. And she talked about men using her. Some Hollywood type. And a writer or a critic," Israel most likely.[16]

In 1969 Allan and Diane divorced, another major stressor. As Arbus explained to a friend, "I guess it was oddly enough the finality of Allan leaving (for Calif.) that so shook me . . . Suddenly it was no more pretending. This was it."[17] Allan now away, at least physically—he continued to send money on occasion—Diane transferred her emotional attachment even more fiercely onto Marvin Israel.

Rage became more and more of a problem. Israel was siphoning off his attentions. As a friend said, "She expected others to do for her constantly, and when they didn't, her irritation was profound."[18] The hostility extended to Israel's wife, whom Arbus envied. More or less self-punishingly, according to Bosworth, Diane took to standing in the shadows outside the Israels' studio, where she would wait for either of them to emerge. A sculptor, Nancy Grossman, introduced to Arbus by Marvin Israel, comments on her labile moods: "Some days, when she was up, she looked and acted like a very young girl. Other days, when she was depressed, her face would resemble an old, old woman."[19]

It was during this period that Arbus entered therapy with Boigon. Other physicians Arbus consulted prescribed minor tranquilizers such as the then popular Librium, but she resisted taking them in light of what was regarded as a "bad reaction" to Vivactil.[20] Money was an issue too. She was doing a lot of lecturing—something she didn't always enjoy—and taking pictures for various magazines, such as the shot of Borges in Central Park for *Harper's Bazaar*.

In spring of 1969 Arbus visited her mentor Lisette Model. Arbus struck Model then as especially girlish and anxious, almost regressed. Model later remarked on Arbus's tendency to make "obsessive demands that cannot be satisfied," most of these centering on people in her life.[21]

Arbus moved into Westbeth in early 1970, an artists' community near the Hudson River. Her spirits lifted temporarily. As one resident put it, "every artist [there] was going through some kind of crisis," so Arbus's misery found company. In fact, she always believed good art had to be hard. If it wasn't hard, it wasn't any good.

It was also in 1970, roughly one year prior to her suicide, that Arbus began to take photos of the mentally retarded at a home in Vineland, New Jersey. A distinctive feature of special importance concerns the subjects of such shots: They paid little attention to the photographer. Absorbed simply in what they were doing, they seemed to Arbus virtually selfless. There were no masks to vitiate artfully. Thus, as subjects, the retarded were not like anyone Arbus had ever photographed before. Simultaneous with this new development in her work, Arbus began offering her photography master class as a way of making money that might be used to buy a new camera, a Pentax, which ran around a thousand dollars. The class was difficult for her in the sense that she felt no affinity for the work of the students; she needed to do a fair amount of insincere encouraging. "After each class I think, whew . . . but that's a hard act to follow."[22]

In early 1971 Arbus started work on a series for a Time-Life Books on the topic, promisingly, of love. For this she took the shot of a New Jersey housewife—Mrs. Gladys Ulrich—with a baby macaque monkey named Sam that she dressed in ridiculous clothing. If this was love, it was love of a particularly misguided kind. There had been a previous Sam, another monkey, but as Arbus explains in her caption for the photo, "the original Sam hung himself by accident."[23] Arbus called the picture "Madonna and Child," and what she said about it speaks volumes: The woman was "extremely serious and grave holding her monkey, the same way you'd be grave about the safety of a child." Another shot taken around the same time, this one not for Time-Life Books, was the famous albino sword-swallower picture that likewise makes religious allusions—the woman's body, combined with the vertical sword, forms a cross.

Two suicides occurred at Westbeth in spring 1971. In one case a photographer jumped from the roof. In response Arbus told a friend that she, too, had thought of suicide, but couldn't entertain the idea seriously because it would mean an end to her work, which was all that really mattered. The work must go on.

In May 1971, two months before her suicide, *Artforum* published a portfolio of Arbus's pictures along with her dream about the sinking ocean liner on which she was a passenger, shooting pictures elatedly. The *Artforum* piece arrived on the heels of various trivial tensions, most revolving around money.[24] *Harper's Bazaar* initially refused to pay her expenses in Germany for a session with Bertolt Brecht's widow, Helene Weigel. She refers to "sudden money panic." She finds she owes eighteen hundred dollars, "not counting normal next month bills and taxes." She says "this is the point at which I usually get sick."[25] She also was invited by Walker Evans to teach a photography class at Yale, but she declined. She had a hard time believing she was deserving of such opportunities. Because of her depression, she felt incapable of carrying them out. She was taking pictures now of bondage houses. She meets a one-armed man, a leading figure in the S&M community, the one who thought of his stump as a "potent phallic symbol."[26]

To Lisette Model, Arbus confided that the photos of the mentally retarded no longer made any sense to her. This was June 1971, one month before her suicide. She now hated the pictures. She told friends her art was not doing it for her anymore. She was not getting anything back from it. It no longer met her needs.[27] Later in June she took the pictures of Germaine Greer, who described Arbus as tyrannical: "I felt completely terrorized by the blasted lens . . . This frail rosepetal creature kept at me like a laser beam."[28] A friend notes: "We didn't know how to deal with her. It was excruciatingly depressing to be with her. She would drag you down—she would bore you."[29] Others describe her as "thinking too fast": "she talked very fast, all in a rush."

From June 20 to 27 Arbus actually managed a class at Hampshire College that she refers to as "horrible." Model saw her yet again and this time found her surprisingly "beautiful and strong . . . Not one wrinkle. Brown. Young-looking."[30]

On July 10, severely distraught, Arbus visited the loft of two female friends. She was exhausted and crying. The work on the pictures of the mentally retarded had drained her completely. At one point Arbus said to the two women, "I wish I could go to bed with both of you," duplicating her comment to the Kronhausens several years earlier. She was desperately in need of comforting. As usual, sexual intimacy suggested itself as a sort of panacea. The women were shocked and a little appalled, threatened.[31]

Two weeks later, on the day the Apollo 15 astronauts were launched to the moon, Arbus took her life. On her desk her journal recorded the words "Last Supper" for July 26. Patricia Bosworth contends that Lisette Model received a note but has refused to reveal its contents. Rumors circulated to the effect that Arbus shot her own death—a possibility she had referred to obliquely in a lecture from 1970, during which she told the story of a photographer getting shot, and in that very moment taking a picture of the man with the gun.

She was found by Marvin Israel on July 28. He let himself into the apartment, having been unable to reach her by phone. In the words of the medical investigator's report, she was "crunched up in bath tub, on left side . . . wearing red shirt, blue denim shorts, no socks."[32] Lab findings subsequently showed barbiturate poisoning—amobarbitol and secobarbitol present. Both right and left wrists were cut transversely—three cuts on the left side, two on the right.

Sifting through these facts, one thing becomes depressingly clear: In the months preceding her death, Arbus was a living suicide algorithm. Virtually every single identified risk factor was not only present but strongly present. She was depressed, for starters. There was physical illness, the hepatitis diagnosis of 1968. There was loss of support and rejection, Israel's reluctance to be there for her in the way she felt she needed him, however strange. Her daughters were away—Doon in Paris, Amy at school. Money was a nagging panic, in perilously short supply; Boigon notes that the work Arbus did was a source of irritation, a drag. Divorce was a factor, another loss of a uniquely important attachment object, her husband Allan. Sexuality figures. According to instruments estimating suicide risk, bisexuality or promiscuity both increase overall probability. Rage and aggression elevate risk, too, and several sources, Boigon especially, cite Arbus's anger. Even a few impersonal elements might have played some role. Suicide is higher in hot summer months like July, when Arbus died. And there's the so-called contagion effect, the two other suicides at Westbeth increasing the idea's prominence.[33]

The only powerful single predictor not present in Arbus's case is alcoholism or drug use. Plus, most successful suicides follow on the heels of suicide talk or preparation—planning—and a history of prior attempts. Arbus made occasional references to suicide, but never in the form of a real intention, and never in the course of her therapy. With Boigon the idea simply didn't come up. It wasn't on the radar. And there were no practice runs—no so-called "suicide gestures," no parasuicidal behavior of any sort. In this respect Arbus's death was a mild rarity. She tried suicide just once, and she succeeded, whether she actually meant to or not.

So, entering these objective factors into a sort of risk equation makes Arbus's death less "perplexing," more "intelligible," in reference to the position of the estate. But personality's more than a rubric. And as Kafka once put it, "Nothing alive can be calculated." In the end some fraction of mystery, some blurriness, always remains. There are ambiguities, empty cells in the calculus, uncertainties to deal with. One can't isolate *the cause* of Arbus's suicide, not because causes don't exist—they do, in an ultimate sense—but because they can't be pinpointed with certainty. This isn't an experiment, after all. It is possible, however, to explore more deeply a handful of factors especially active in the overall gestalt of motives behind Arbus's action.

We can start at adolescence. By this time Arbus was depressed; her autobiography makes that fact plain. Her mother was also depressed—cut-off, feeling like a "zombie." Therefore, even before adulthood, Arbus needed to evolve some means of dealing with the reality of depressed moods and correlated anxieties, in short "negative affect." For her, because of obvious gifts in this domain, art became the solution, or at least *one* solution among others. Art was a way of exploring the depression, externalizing it in pictures, containing it, maybe even understanding or reversing it, in the best of instances. She made her subjects look as angry and alone and depressed and anxious as she was. They recorded her feelings. She created a visual world that reflected her and, in the process, consoled her. As a solution art must have succeeded to some degree because from the moment she struck out on her own as an artist, the taking of pictures instantly became compulsive. She needed her work. She couldn't live without it. It even became her reason for living, as she explains when discussing the lure of suicide. For a time, at least, her position seems to have been that she must go on because the work must go on. The work made her life valuable. She had to make the sacrifice, so to speak, of continuing to live.

In a 1968 letter to a friend, Arbus explains how the very idea of depression left her terrified. "Energy . . . just leaks out and I am left lacking the confidence even to cross the street."[34] This observation was made around the same time Arbus first tried antidepressants. It could be that the Vivactil had iatrogenic effects—it perhaps worsened the depression and anxiety, caused generalized agitation. She talks about going up and down a lot. She gets "filled with energy and joy," begins to think about what she wants to do, feels "all breathless with excitement," but then suddenly, mysteriously, the energy "vanishes," leaving her "harassed, swamped, distraught, frightened."[35] The fear is important. She'd had those tortured-artist fantasies, but the reality of the sadness, its fearsomeness, couldn't be easily romanticized. Art was the primary palliative, but so were relationships, sex, and the prospect of psychotherapy. A lot of what Arbus did, especially in the last years of her life, was anxiety motivated and counterphobic. She feared rejection, no doubt, but she also feared depression, and she did what was necessary to muzzle it. Even the study of freaks or eccentrics, according to a book by Edith Sitwell that Arbus read closely, can keep swirling melancholies at arm's length.

There was rage to deal with, too, a lot of it traceable to disappointment with lovers: attachment-figure unresponsiveness. The rage had a tantrumy quality to it, a regressiveness implying a system in full red alert; it recalls the hate Arbus referenced when friends failed to keep her secrets or didn't return her love in the intense, flawless way she wanted them to. During her convalescence she talks about not knowing how to make the "werewolf" rage "energy." It's a key observation. I think she *did* actually know, at least unconsciously, how to make rage energy. It was a motor of her art, a motive insufficiently recognized in analyses of her work. She always made a point of saying how much she loved and "adored" her freak subjects, and in some cases she probably did. But these expressions can also be defensive, a way of denying darker currents of feeling. She aggressively seduced her sitters, dominated them, made them look how she wanted them to. They wound up feeling manipulated, confused, betrayed—"Arbused." In short, they say they were deceived.

The shots of Germaine Greer exemplify this dynamic perfectly. Savvier than most, Greer knew what Arbus was up to. But Arbus performed a similar confidence trick with Mae West, who was "furious" when her pictures appeared, and with Jacqueline Susann and her husband, Irving Mansfield, who called Arbus bossy. "She made us move all over the place," Mansfield said. "Then she wanted us to pose in our bathing suits next to the TV set. I didn't get it, so I said no to the idea, but Jackie . . . said of course . . . Particularly after Arbus had assured us this shot would be for her portfolio—*not for publication* . . . We held the pose for what seemed like hours . . . Arbus looked tense . . . She'd flown out specifically to photograph us and she seemed a little angry about it."[36]

But photographers do this. They know what they want, for personal and artistic reasons, and it doesn't always accord with what their subjects want. One has to be ruthless. And it's possible to argue that, without such manipulations, about which Diane was aware, the work would suffer. Anger is useful to creativity. Some artists are simply angry, and so is their art. For Arbus, however—and this is the case for other artists as well—the anger was tangled up with depression. It surfaced but then got turned inward, against the self. Its objects, in other words, were external and internal. Hate was there, but so was self-hatred, suicide's inevitable ally.

Arbus's session with Viva, the "Superstar at Home," is a model instance of hate and self-hate joining forces bitterly, to the art's detriment, if not Arbus's too. Viva had been an actress in a number of Warhol films such as *Blue Movie, aka Fuck* and

Lonesome Cowboy, where she appeared nude "and talking nonstop while participating in an orgy and a masturbation scene." (The orgy and masturbation details provide a path of identification for Arbus.) Diane met her in her filthy apartment. Later she and Arbus got stoned on hash, Viva says, and Diane took pictures of her having sex with an actor and his wife. Later Arbus had Viva lie on a couch naked and roll her eyes up at the ceiling—a shot that was published. Viva declares, "Those photographs were totally faked. They were planned and manipulated. Diane Arbus lied, cheated, and victimized me. She said she was just going to take head shots. I trusted her because she acted like a martyr, a little saint, about the whole thing," just as she did with Jack Dracula and countless others, no doubt.[37]

Patricia Bosworth calls the images "absolutely merciless" and "brutal."[38] She notes a "seeming disregard for the subject," not particularly new for Arbus. The pictures when they appeared threatened *New York* magazine's advertising. There was "much mail and cancelled subscriptions," Arbus says, many pro and con phone calls. Viva pursued a lawsuit that eventually was dropped.[39] It's interesting: Arbus sees the accompanying article as "harsh and humorless," but not the pictures, which she finds "fascinating." Arbus's sister Renee says she told her she took the shots deliberately as a means of making more money; she thought sensationalistic pictures would lead to additional assignments. But there was a lot more at work psychologically. Arbus identified with Viva, just as she had with Penelope Tree, who also despised the results of their sessions. In looking at Viva what Arbus saw was a florid version of herself, a pitiful, disgusting self-image. Like Arbus, Viva came from an unhappy home (her father's favorite expressions being "shut up" and "cross your legs"), used sex to combat depression, and was in thrall to men who controlled her emotions. As Viva said about Warhol, "He just gets you and you can't get away. Now I can't make the simplest decision or go anywhere without asking Andy."[40] This all took place in spring of 1968, when Arbus was at her most depressed.

For Arbus, photography had to be hard. One had to pay a price for the motives behind the work. One had to suffer. Far more than anything else, as she said again and again, Arbus regarded photography as naughty. In part this had to do with the obvious sexual aspect of her work; but it also had to do with how she used it surreptitiously and maybe mostly unconsciously to manipulate people into enacting her private fear and anger, her self-loathing.

Germaine Greer, in a 2005 article for the *Guardian*, revisited her Arbus shoot.[41] It's not a fond remembrance. First of all, she dismisses the "nonsense" about Arbus's "empathy with her subjects." Mirrored on the faces of most of her sitters, Greer contends, is "faint bewilderment and timid resentment." Arbus "neither knew nor cared who they were," never allowing any of her subjects to simply "look good." What she pursued was pain, discomfort, embarrassment, irritation—anything but prettiness or aplomb. Greer goes on: "Throughout the session she spoke very little and always in a deceptively apologetic murmur . . . I understood that as soon as I exhibited any signs of distress, she would have her picture. She would get behind the public persona of *Life* cover-girl Germaine Greer, the 'sexy feminist that men like.'" The short piece concludes: "The emotion that thrills through every Arbus icon making them haunting and unforgettable is a relentless, all-encompassing loathing . . . Arbus's creativity was driven by disgust . . . Good haters can make good art, but their despair and indignation ought to be called forth by something more sinister than mere human imperfection and self-delusion." In other words, Arbus seized on prosaic flaws as a way of liberating her own disgust and hatred. There was something outsized and self-indulgent about what she was up to.

A critically important fact about suicide, often overlooked entirely, is this: It's *self-murder.* It's a response to what suicidologist Edwin Shneidman calls "psychache," the pain of living, but its energy is transformed hate. We kill what we despise *in ourselves.* We murder internalized fragments. One way out is through the use of external targets on which rage can be made to exhaust itself, an avenue Arbus was trying unconsciously to explore. But for whatever reason, it didn't work. Either the targets—like Susann, Viva, Tree, and Greer—were somehow unsuitable, or the rage was too intense, too abundant.

It's here where the shots of the mentally retarded take on special significance. At first Arbus adored the pictures. They shored her up; they released a kindness and love that was always there but unreliable, in fragile supply, elbowed aside by anger. Psychologist Melanie Klein connects this sort of cultivation of good objects to idealization, a defense against anxiety. Arbus fortified her own limited cache of internal goodness by making the retarded into absurdly gratifying figures. She filled notebooks with observations—the time they played Simon Says in a field or formed a circle for running in place. She lists physical characteristics—Carmela is fat and cross-eyed, Nancy slightly bearded, Barbara sweet and bright, Phyllis a "solemn intelligent mongoloid."[42]

But then, inevitably, as the end of her life loomed, she hated them—the shots, at least. They were fool's gold. Her work, she confided, was not "working" for her anymore. And the horrifying meaning of such a realization quickly dawned—without her work "doing it," she could not survive.

What is it about these shots that so unnerved Arbus? Several things. First of all, these were people beyond manipulation. In their selflessness they could not be used, seduced, exposed. There was no mask, no persona, no falseness for Arbus to aggressively sweep away through the magic denuding of the camera. In short, these were people Arbus could not hate. They were defenseless, innocent. And so, to the degree that anger was something Arbus was getting out of her photography, there would be no getting of that here. Rage was left to identify a different target, and where it coalesced was around the self. It returned to its source.

Another element concerns the mirroring function of Arbus's pictures. These subjects did not look back as others had done before. They did not react or participate. If what Arbus was hunting was a confirmation of self, a way of forcing people to see her into being, there was slim chance of that with the mentally retarded. It was a function they were ill suited to serve. Arbus was left with a lonely, empty feeling. She was thrown back on the one thing that remained—herself. And given the colossal importance of other people in her life, of whom she tended to make incessant demands, this wasn't a happy place to be. In fact, it was a dangerous place. With the retarded, what Arbus was in the business of interrogating was a virtual void, and when the void looked back, when she saw it in the pictures, it conveyed her own blankness, the "nothing" Colin Wood, the boy with the hand grenade, spoke of.

Arbus feared depression, she feared fear, but she also feared numbness. She feared the blankness, the nothing. As Boigon put it, what she was after was experience, only experience, something to fill her up. Two ways she found this experience, defeated the blankness, revolved around sex and relationships. These, too, are factors of extreme importance when it comes to Arbus's suicide. We already explored the role of attachment insecurity in Arbus's early life. It's absolutely key. In times of emotional distress she pursued people who served a mitigating function. At age fourteen she found one she foreclosed on with absolute fervor: Allan Arbus. In 1969 Allan was gone, off to Hollywood. With him went a new wife. This departure fomented Arbus's "obsession," as many have called it, with Marvin Israel. But the Israel relationship brought up old wounds and dynamics, since he was married and not as automatically responsive as Arbus needed him to be, according to Bosworth. (I should add: I am speaking of her emotional needs, not her artwork; the latter Israel obviously strongly supported.) She made him a substitute attachment figure, but he resisted the role. She became enraged. Boigon notes how rage at Israel was a constant theme of the therapy, right down to the last days of Arbus's life. Amidst all this Arbus was compulsively seeking out sex with strangers—orgies and people she met on the street. Boigon tells us that these strangers were often repellent figures—"ugly and odd-appearing."

Sex helped Arbus fend off depression, feelings of being insufficiently loved and cared for. It provided temporary relief, reversed numbness. But random sex in particular is attachment's opposite. One has it, one moves on. The stranger remains a stranger. There's no comfort to be had. But Arbus frantically kept at it, even targeting "queer-looking" people. The self-disgust this implies is obvious. It's an incredibly self-punishing agenda, doomed to fail miserably—a painful, self-defeating revolving door. Sex brought immediate, intense closeness, briefly addressing emotional needs; but disgust soon followed, then self-loathing, then more depression, leading to more sexual desperation. That Arbus in the last days of her life suggested climbing into bed with two female friends is unsurprising. This was how she coped. It was her pattern, long since established. Marvin Israel was now unresponsive, Allan Arbus on the West Coast, a country away. The women had one thing going for them—they were there. And Arbus's needs were unrelenting.

Another small detail clearly related to the function of men in Arbus's life and her need for mollifying relationships is the dream of the mad scientist. Arbus asks him to tell her what is wrong with her and how he proposes to cure it. But he pretends not to hear and strides off. He is nine feet tall, a sort of monster. Larger than life, he's the giant who can save her, a grotesque daddy figure. But he won't listen; he won't respond. He keeps "outdistancing" her. A crucial realization emerges: He has "discovered a cure that kills people"—in other words, the solution he offers is no solution at all. He then turns shadowlike, "black like a silhouette." He splits into lots of little men scurrying off in different directions; there is "no way of knowing whom to pursue." Arbus concludes: "You are dead when you ask the doctor why you are sick and he doesn't hear you."

This seems like a perfect little allegory for Arbus's relationship history. Huge men who do not hear, scurrying off in different directions, the question of which one to pursue, each of them promising a cure that kills—it's all there, the unreliability, the unresponsiveness, the desperate need to seek a connection that can't really satisfy in the end. Even the phoniness of the father makes an appearance. The giant promises something he refuses to deliver on.

One last point about the role of relationships in Arbus's life relates to Boigon's use of the term "schizoid" to describe her. I see Arbus as high in the far less pathological trait of openness, her style of thinking more creative than disturbed. The writing she did, for instance, whether in her notebooks, in letters, in grant applications, or in published text accompanying photographs, is brilliantly original. In it one sees a very fluid, fast, original mind working at high speed. She was a photographer, but she was also a writer. The talent was astonishingly developed in her. But schizoid has to do not only with mental organization, with the form thought takes; it includes, even more importantly, styles of relating. Such people typically come across as aloof and isolative, locked away, internally preoccupied. They are highly sensitive and reactive to personal stimulation. Because they fear being engulfed, enmeshed, controlled, and traumatized—dangers they associate with other people—their tendency is to retreat to the fantasy life of their minds. They move away from others. They seclude themselves. But less commonly, some schizoid individuals feel a yearning for closeness and have elaborate fantasies about emotional and sexual intimacy that tend to get communicated via metaphor and emotionally meaningful references to literature, music, and the arts.

It's a formidable dilemma. What they fear they also need—people. Closeness entails vulnerability. It's a high-risk gamble—dependency and love are dangerous—but secretly, in his or her walled-off fantasy universe, the schizoid person moves toward others, not away.

R.D. Laing said people feared three things: death, their own minds, and other people. Though Arbus rarely spoke of death, her work reveals a fascination. She took pictures in morgues, shot her own dead grandmother, her father in his hospital bed weeks before he died of lung cancer. And her mind was her power. It was a source of pleasure. Her moods and anxieties raked her, her sense of identity hung by a thread, but her intellect, the acuity of her perceptions, her capacity to see what no one else could or would—those abilities rarely failed her. They sustained her, in fact. It was other people, always other people, who gave Arbus problems. Shooting them was research. It was very psychological. She wanted to know, for instance, whether Polly Bushong—the woman who, in her spare time, dressed up as the preposterous Cora Pratt—really had two selves inside her. She wanted to know how sincere freaks actually were: Was their act authentic or phony? Other people were Arbus's drug of choice. From adolescence on, she needed everything they could give her; she swallowed them up, but rarely without distrust, gnawing dissatisfaction. At the end others found her needs repellent. She was impossible to take, impossible to be around. As Model told her, it was essential she let go of "obsessive demands that cannot be satisfied." The mad-scientist dream says it all: Men scurried off in different directions, and anyway, the cure they offered killed you. You couldn't live without it, but if you got it, you died.

In the last half year of Arbus's life—1971—she was teaching at Hampshire College in Amherst. A shot by W.T. Graham shows her in June, a month before her death, frozen mid-sentence, looking thin, tired, beat, but mentally alive, engaged. She shot the June wedding of Richard Nixon's daughter, Tricia—"a paper doll"—and found being searched by the FBI great fun "because you knew you were innocent."[43] There was the session with Greer, a photo of a blonde girl with a hot dog, a young man in a trench coat, a woman passing by on the street with hat, fur collar, and purse, an image, like so many others by Arbus, of lonely-looking middle-aged females—at drugstore counters, on buses, in high-ceilinged hotel rooms—left to their own devices, left to fend for themselves.

The scant published facts make for more questions than answers. The words "Last Supper" were written on July 26, apparently in the evening, two days before Arbus was found dead. It's an improbably religious allusion, referring, of course, to the final meal Jesus shared with his twelve apostles and disciples. Taking the wine and bread, Jesus tells his followers: "Do this in remembrance of me." He then reveals the event's most memorable detail, a coming betrayal. The Gospel of Mark does not name the betrayer, nor does Luke. Only Matthew and John single out Judas Iscariot. The meal finished, Jesus delivers a large sermon in which he defines the greatest love as laying down one's life for one's friends, a passage since used to affirm the sacrifice of martyrs and soldiers at war.

Arbus wasn't religious. What she knew about the meaning of the words "Last Supper" is unknown. It could have been an arbitrary notation; it could have been much more. Jesus, of course, allowed himself to be killed in order to free mankind from sin. But with specific reference to Arbus, the notion of laying down one's life for one's friends as an act of great love and selflessness aligns with a model of suicide, Joiner's Interpersonal-Psychological theory, according to which "suicidal people are specifically hopeless about feelings of being a burden on others and of failed belongingness."[44] Dying, it's felt, relieves others of responsibility. It's an act of generosity, of mercy, a sacrificial gesture. With death, the person's unreasonable demands disappear, sparing others the burdensomeness of providing care. Ideas like these easily could have been on Arbus's mind. She had become a bit of a burden, difficult to be around, inconsolably needy.

Arbus certainly felt betrayed—in part by her art, but mainly by Israel's perceived abandonment. Days before, he'd spent a long weekend with his wife at Fire Island in the home of Richard Avedon. He was away, and he wasn't alone. Any time Israel spent with his wife was time taken from Diane, and her condition was such that she needed people and their time, their affection, more than ever.

The full meaning of "Last Supper" Arbus may have spelled out: She may have said exactly what it meant to her. As far as can be determined, however, no one knows whether she did or not, since two additional pages from the appointment book, covering July 27 and July 28, were "meticulously excised," according to the Arbus estate. The appointment book appears otherwise perfectly intact, but with the pages in question "no longer in it." They have "never been recovered," the estate maintains. "Presumably" the medical investigator took them, or "someone else in authority."[45]

These missing pages are the crowning mystery in a mysterious, secret-choked life. It's ironic: Arbus's last confession was denied her. But by whom? Israel found Arbus some time in the evening. While there in the apartment he got in touch with three friends—Larry Shainberg, Jay Gold, and Richard Avedon—who each came to help.[46] Then the police were notified, the medical investigator arriving on the scene at nine forty-five, "about two and a half hours after official notification." The "Last Supper" note was submitted for study. Why weren't the other two pages? Under what kind of scenario could they have been misplaced after being so "meticulously" excised? Why, in other words, does the "Last Supper" note survive but not the July 27 and July 28 material?

Coroner reports are not publicly available. Only next of kin can access them. So the family alone knows the complete facts. One possibility is that Israel excised the pages, not the medical examiner. He was alone in the apartment for a decent period of time, maybe several hours. There would have been ample opportunity. And there might have been reason, depending on what the missing pages said exactly. In any case, suicide notes are treated appropriately gravely, carefully. They don't generally disappear into thin air. If anything from the scene was collected and kept with extraordinary care, the missing pages were. That one page survives while the other two do not makes very little sense under the circumstances. Simply put, it's hard to believe. But if anyone ever knew differently, they didn't say, or aren't saying, or aren't presently alive to say.

A fact unearthed by Patricia Bosworth is particularly interesting and more than a little morbid. Some time in June 1971, Arbus assisted Israel in the completion of a sculpture "of a person of no specific sex lying on a bed." Bosworth says the person's wrists are "obviously slashed"—both of them.[47] It's yet another suicide scenario, like others in Israel's very bizarre, very disturbing corpus. Arbus's manner of death, the fact that she cut both her wrists, references this sculpture, and therefore Israel too, possibly intentionally. Cutting both wrists is difficult to do. First, it requires the use of a non-dominant hand. Second, it's extremely painful, far more than most people typically assume. The pain itself, in fact, often leads a person to stop, thereby saving his or her life.

Images of the sculpture in question are impossible to come by. It isn't certain that it was ever completed. But there are at least two other visible Israel works from 1971, the year of Arbus's death. Both focus on sex repulsively. One shows a woman sitting on a man's lap, facing the viewer squarely. The man has no face; it's a swirling, circling series of black lines resembling a tornado. He's in a suit. The woman is expressionless in a polka-dotted blouse and knee-length boots, her hair parted in the middle. The man's right hand slips under the blouse, onto the woman's left breast. The woman's legs are spread, and both she and the man fondle her vagina.

The other image is framed identically, with a chair in the center of the composition. This time a dog sits in the chair panting and snarling. It looks legless, its erect penis and two testicles displayed vividly. Scattered across the floor are heeled women's shoes and another far smaller dog that appears dead.

The sculpture implicates Arbus directly—she helped work on it, and her mode of death symbolically duplicates its subject matter. The other two works may have nothing to do with Arbus; it's not clear whether they were made before or after she died. But the strange, repellent sex theme, deliberately vulgar and off-putting, recalls the assorted sex games Arbus and Israel were involved in, according to Boigon's report.

Whatever the case, it was an exceedingly dangerous, emotionally explosive dyad. Chances are Arbus anticipated Israel finding her—dead or alive—and seeing the results of the pain he had caused. Her rage in therapy was directed almost exclusively at Israel. It was intense, Boigon says, and unrelenting; a wish to cause hurt therefore makes sense. This was Boigon's belief, in fact—that Arbus aimed to "punish" Israel, to be found alive and "restored." It was the main idea Boigon wanted to convey to me. She was adamant. And she recalls telling Amy Arbus, Diane's second daughter, the same thing.

Superficially, what Boigon says, especially the notion that Arbus expected to be found alive, seems untenable. Arbus both slit her wrists and swallowed two different barbiturates, amobarbitol and secobarbitol, suggesting an obvious intent to die. But it's more complex than this. The drugs are sedative-hypnotics, not used much anymore in America, but they also have potentially high analgesic properties. They reduce pain, in other words. My guess is that Arbus took the medicines to dull the pain of cutting, not in order to overdose. She had never cut herself before, and so she had no means of anticipating how cutting would feel—how excruciatingly painful it would be—particularly when the cuts are deep. Taking amobarbitol and secobarbitol does not, in itself, imply intent to die. The motive might have been pain reduction, a way of making cutting possible.

A number of studies exist looking at acute barbiturate poisoning and death. In one investigation covering more than one hundred cases over a two-year span, mortality rate was a mere 0.8 percent. One can suicide using barbiturates, but it isn't usually a successful method. A lot depends on drug amount, and also on the precise barbiturate employed. Amobarbitol is classified as

an intermediate-acting substance, with two to four hours duration of action. Most typically, it produces coma at eight to twelve
milligrams per hundred milliliters. Secobarbitol is short-acting,
more dangerous. Its duration of action is fifteen minutes to
three hours, and it brings about coma at two to four milligrams
per hundred milliliters. According to the autopsy report reproduced, apparently fully, in *Revelations*, Arbus's barbiturate level
was 3.45 milligrams. There are cases in the literature in which
patients survived with levels of 11.2, 13.25, and 21.3, respectively.[48]
Arbus's liver was congested, likely because of her hepatitis, so
that's a factor to take into account; but even so, a barbiturate level
of 3.45 achieved by a combination of amobarbitol—intermediate-
acting—and secobarbitol—short-acting—is survivable. It isn't
likely that the overdose killed Diane Arbus. It's possible, not
probable.

Wrist cutting also has a low fatality rate of 4 to 6 percent. It
accounts for only 1.5 percent of completed suicides, more effective methods being firearms, hanging, and poisoning—92.3
percent of completed suicides include the use of one of these
three methods, firearms associated with the highest degree of
mortality.[49] Superficial cutting is surprisingly common, especially nowadays, and it tends to be "parasuicidal." Rarely lethal,
it can constitute a so-called "cry for help," an attempt at manipulation eliciting responsiveness, or in some chronic cases a
distraction from emotional pain that becomes almost addictive
and therefore very difficult to treat. Arbus's cuts were not superficial. They were "deep," they "severed many tendons," but left
"veins on both sides intact." The hands were covered by a large
amount of blood, also the "anterior aspects of the lower legs,
below the knees." She was found in the bath, but there's no

information about the presence of warm or hot water, which could have facilitated bleeding.

Boigon's position on the cutting is that Arbus had no realistic sense of what she was doing, no understanding of potential lethality. She'd never cut before, for one thing. There was no past history to draw on. She also, according to Boigon, had very little facility for "scientific" thinking. It's unlikely, Boigon says, that Arbus planned the act, researched it in any way, thought it through, or possessed the ability to predict the outcome of what she was engaged in. She was behaving impulsively, in other words, not planfully or with deliberate intent. Her success was accidental, not the product of forethought.

In the end, intent is guesswork. Risk factors were strongly present but impersonal, as always; alone they say nothing about the real desire to die. Arbus was very angry, and according to friends inconsolably needy. She was in pain and she was desperate. Cutting is self-punishment, the expression of hate directed at the body. Self-harm punishes others, too, in this instance the people whom Arbus felt let her down, dismissed her needs, failed to pay attention. Arbus was adept at getting others to respond to her, friends and subjects. This time, however, all the usual strategies failed. So what she did was try an unusual strategy, one not resorted to before. If there was intentionality in the suicidal behavior, the goal was to elicit support, to make people care and respond. What Arbus was after, most likely, was what she was always after—love. It was an extreme way of trying to get it, but then her needs were extreme too. It's possible that, like a lot of suicide attempters, she didn't care in the moment whether she lived or died. She wanted the pain to stop.

Not the life, but the pain. What she didn't know, what she couldn't predict, was that stopping one might end the other.

The English writer Martin Amis once said this about suicide: "The murderer kills just one person; the suicide kills everybody." He refers to it as "omnicide," calls it a "worldkiller." These ideas recall Wittgenstein's: "If suicide is allowed, then everything is allowed." Suicide, Wittgenstein says, is therefore "the elementary sin." When one investigates it, it is "like investigating mercury vapour in order to comprehend the nature of vapours." I do think Arbus was up to worldkilling, her feeling along the lines of *"This cannot go on."* There is rage against the self, obvious self-hatred in the act, treating the self as an enemy, but there's also rage against the world, against the people in it who cause, intentionally or not, harm. Suicide destroys thoroughly. It is a wiping out of everything. Arbus wanted the present to end—it was unbearable, grueling, her situation irremediable—but I'm not sure she wanted the future to end too. It's paradoxical, but so are many essential truths. Suicide's about pain and anger; it's not mathematics. Arbus's wish was to start fresh, start over, erase the given. If she'd lived, this wish might have been granted. But she overshot the mark. It was success and failure combined. She killed the world, but she killed herself too. She wanted the former to happen; I don't believe she wanted the latter.

Chapter 7

THE HOLE IN THE GROUND
WHERE SECRETS LIVED

A RBUS MEANS FREAKS. Arbus means sex. Arbus means self, identical opposites like the New Jersey twins. But most of all, Arbus means secrets. Photography was a private sin, the photograph a secret about a secret. The fourteen-year-old Arbus needed to confide, to get things out; her adult photography is a long, unlovely confession. There was always some sense in which she identified with her subjects, saw herself in them, so the shots themselves are revelations. What she *told* others as a fourteen-year-old she *shows* as an adult. It was never easy for Arbus to take in reactions to the pictures. Acclaim in particular unnerved her, left her shaky, besieged, paranoid. That's because people weren't simply responding to images; they were judging her subjective life. She was the shot. She was part of the meaning.

In the 1950s a distinctly confessional poetry emerged out of the writing of Robert Lowell and others. It was liberating. The normally suppressed territory of the self—unvarnished, ugly— found declarative voice. Sylvia Plath, Lowell's student, seized on this possibility and made poems compressing a dark, scary, formless, and virtually psychotic interior. There's no indication Arbus read Plath or knew her life story. She wouldn't have; Plath's fame postdated Arbus's suicide. The biographies didn't come until many years later. But there's a strong affinity. Arbus's work was just as confessional, just as hard, just as not-nice. And of course both lives took the same road, allowing no one-eighty.

Psychologists writing about art and creativity make a distinction between defensive and restitutive functions.[1] Conceptually, it's an easy bifurcation; in the messy details of the life itself, not so much. The question is: Does the art merely rehearse and reinstate wounds, or does it allow for catharsis and working through, does it become therapeutic? The latter idea—art as therapy—is a commonplace. The notion that creativity soothes fears, lessens anxiety, forms formlessness, puts a poultice on depression is entrenched in the culture. It's taken as intrinsic, axiomatic. It even influences therapy—if the patient is trauma afflicted, then have her write the trauma out, encase it in anxiety-dispatching words.

To me, reality's far less rosy. Flashback dreams repeat trauma, force unwanted re-viewings that don't make for happy returns. Art as waking dream can do the same. It sometimes puts the trauma right in your face, front and center. It's more reminder than redemption. It forces a confrontation already implicit, and it involves whoever sees the work or reads it. In these cases there's no confession booth, no shielding, soundproof walls. The whole congregation gets implicated.

The thrill in looking closely at an Arbus picture or, for that matter, reading a Plath poem is a fear of the dark. We've been there, too, it's never easy going in, but we turn the key anyway.

We can't help it. For Plath, it's clear: We know we are reading poems about the lure of suicide. We also know the writer did not survive them. She died for the art and the price was worth it. She bought genius. She couldn't get it any other way.

The same calculus applies to Arbus. We follow her into haunted houses. She's our Virgil. But the risk we take is purely vicarious. We don't die.

Lisette Model could see Arbus's pathology, her schizophrenia, in every picture. Without it, there is no Arbus. The pathology *was* the genius. For artists like Arbus or Plath, a choice gets made that's instinctive, almost wordless. Make art that's natural and risky, that burns, wounds, and confesses, or make art that's unnatural and tame, with affect flattened. Plath took both these roads. Her early work, *The Colossus*, for instance, was elegant, formal, stately, obscure. But it was also bloodless, withheld. *Ariel* was a dismantling. If poetry's a taming, then *Ariel* wasn't even poetry. It splattered on the page like a Pollock drip painting. It was anything but bloodless, and it was genius. It was genius because of the blood.

Arbus took just one road. Rarely is anything withheld in her work. The risk, then, was greater, or at least more constant. The art had a *sameness* to it, what Shelley Rice calls an "*insistent* sameness" reflective of Arbus's "personal trauma." What one keeps encountering is an "essential void," naïve, simplistic, manipulative of the pictures' subjects. The point of view is unrelievedly subjective. Rice, of course, sees this as a flaw. She contrasts Arbus's subjective art with Model's restrained, classical objectivity. It's the difference between *Ariel* and *The Colossus*. But being more Model wasn't an option for Arbus any more than being more Arbus was an option for Model. Besides, there already was a Model. All affinities aside—and there were many—Arbus had to shift the emphasis.

Model looked out, Arbus looked in, and when the artist looks in, takes what's there, and uses it, it's never anything but a refinding. There's going to be a sameness because one discovers the same interior over and over again, the same content, the same raw material. This sameness, the stuckness, the endless recycling—that's the neurotic core. That's the pathology, the repetition. Arbus kept dipping into her subjective well, the hole in the ground where secrets lived, then transposing what she saw there into images. The images were her. Rice wishes they were *more than* her, independent of her, irreducible to her. What the images never managed, Rice claims, was a separate existence.

Some needs, some tendencies—never too clear, usually archaic—recur demonically. It's always there, in all of us, this demonic, and some artists recognize it, welcome it, work in it, while others turn away if they make contact at all. For Freud, the id was the demonic, and what he called the death instinct; for Jung, the demonic was the shadow, an archetype requiring assimilation. It pressed and pressed in one form after another, clamoring to be heard. It had to be confronted, it had to be welcomed in. Confronting it was the only way to silence it.

For Arbus (and Plath, too, in the end), the art was the shadow; for others, it's something else entirely. It comes down to two things: access and usage. For whatever reason, Arbus was gifted with an ability to find and keep secrets. The shadow twin, that enemy within, was an internal presence she knew too well. She acknowledged it and listened to what it had to say. No doubt the gift had something to do with openness, that endogenous tendency Arbus was high in. Openness means low repression; it implies little hard and fast division between levels of conscious-ness. The unconscious permeates day-to-day life more frequently in those who are open; it makes more regular appearances. That also means it's more of a problem. Since it's so often there—on the fringes, but there—it's harder to discount or ignore. Something has to be done with it. A reckoning's re-quired. Other artists don't face the same dilemma. Although it's rare, artists scoring low or midrange on openness do exist. Access to the demonic is, for them, less readily achieved. The secrets stay secret, in a condition of dormancy. The art may unconsciously reference them, but it isn't about them. Most of the time, they repel even inadvertent efforts to get in touch. Arbus was never *not* in touch. She was always handling and try-ing out ways of dealing with powerful, emotion-packed, flam-mable material.

It was the same for Plath. Like Arbus, Plath tried psychother-apy (antidepressants, too, and shock treatment, or what is now called ECT, Electroconvulsive therapy). She began to dream of deformity and death, in reference to her father, Otto Plath, who died when Sylvia was eight, and who in his last months had a leg amputated as a result of untreated diabetes. She also started to access large quantities of rage, most of it centering on a mother whose "eely tentacles" she had described in the poem "Medusa." Plath felt the hate; it was an emotional state she'd succeeded in liberating, and she wondered what to do with it. "What inner decision," she asks herself, "what inner murder or prison-break must I commit if I want to speak from my true deep voice in writing?"[2]

The true deep voice that eventually erupted was a killer. Plath systematically committed poetic murder. Alone with her two small children, in a freezing flat during one of the coldest winters on record, she rose in the early-morning hours while the kids slept and wrote in creative frenzy and literal fever, dealing with temperatures that reached 103. In "Daddy" she killed her father, announcing herself "through" with him; days afterward she killed her mother in "Medusa," saying, "there is nothing between us." Then in the final poems the rage returned to its source. Suicide's a constant theme. Plath made direct contact with her "blacks" that crackled and dragged. It was a subject she says she was "used to." It was always there, an offstage voice, even during the writing of *The Colossus*; but now, having faced the black squarely, Plath identified. She was one with the demonic. The demonic was now unleashed. Like it can do, it took over. To Plath, her submission felt like perfection—"The woman is perfected" she wrote in her last poem, "Edge"—but perfection was an end. There was nowhere to go from it. She had come so far, she said, and "it is over." The poems were the very best she'd ever written. Plath knew it, having said so in a letter to her mother. But she could not survive the making of them.

Jung was shadow obsessed (anima obsessed, too, for different reasons). He wrote in depth about his own "confrontation with the unconscious," a face-off leaving him on the edge of psychosis.[3] He was flooded with visions that he named and communicated with, sometimes according them the status of archetypes. Like Plath and Arbus, Jung turned the night journey into a sort of art—a psychological theory with universal application. There was access and usage. But despite his lifelong fixation on shadow phenomena, the lessons Jung offered were frustratingly tentative. One couldn't exactly assimilate the shadow—that was dangerous, the shadow's power awesome, ageless. To identify was to flirt with disaster. One also couldn't take flight from it—it had to be seen and heard, listened to. Access was a requirement of wholeness of self. Usage was far trickier. Letting the demonic in was one thing; knowing what to do with it once it arrived, another. Jung never figured the problem out. Neither solution worked. The best one could hope for was a kind of detente, the adversaries exhausting themselves in the struggle, agreeing to disagree.

What's most thrilling about Arbus—Plath even more so on account of its precipitousness—is the *descent*, the single-mindedness and tenacity with which she went about it, the fear she overcame. For Arbus the lure started early. The shantytown visit is emblematic, encapsulating the art's motive. She was born into shadow-immunizing wealth that she spent her life painting black. She was a trespasser. She found the forgotten freak and it was assimilated. The repressed returned. Plath, a child of the 1950s, spent most of her early life repressing. The demon took a backseat to surface perfection. Her life was grades, boys, formals, summers at the beach. The bar was set high and she leaped it agilely. The sky was the limit for Sylvia the achiever. But all the while her crackling blacks gathered. Depression reared; there were suicide flirtations and bona fide attempts. One summer she collapsed entirely under all the strain and had to be hospitalized. She wrote about that period in the autobiographical and initially pseudonymous novel *The Bell Jar*. (Her name was disguised because she feared her mother's judgment.) When at last she set the silenced shadow free, putting her art at its disposal, the force was enormous. It engulfed her. She dropped so deeply down, there was no getting up. This drop made her best art possible but it came at a cost she might have willingly paid: her life.

The fact that both Arbus and Plath committed suicide puts a cramp in formulations about their creativity. But setting suicide aside, neither woman had much interest in art as a form of self-mastery. It wasn't, for them, a vehicle for anything other than expression. They wanted the art to be good, not redemptive. And they went where they needed to, did what they had to, to make it good. Arbus, for instance, never discussed her art in therapy and Boigon did not press the subject. It seemed to exist in a parallel universe, private and secret. There was no attempt at integration, no effort to clarify its psychological meaning or function. It just was "not to be explained." For Arbus, picture taking was compulsive. As her brother explained when theorizing about photography in general, it never stopped. But in the hospital she couldn't shoot, and the break felt good. It was a blessing. Arbus went so far as to ask herself, "What if I'm no longer a photographer?" The prospect wasn't entirely unhappy. After all, compulsions of whatever kind don't spell relief; what they signal, by definition, is neurosis. They signal the demonic. Compulsive making of art means unfinished emotional business. Whether Arbus really meant to kill herself or not, the art wasn't allowing her to move beyond or ahead. It wasn't restitutive. Nothing got better. But then, she didn't make art to get better.

Same for Plath. In her journals she never talks about poems coming up in therapy. But unlike Arbus, she did have an interest in the darker origins of her need to write. She was trying to understand where the energy came from. In some ways this was an attempt at *self*-understanding in a broader sense, but that was tangential. What Plath really was after had everything to do with the poems: how to *use* the energy to get the effects she desired, how to *transform* it imaginatively. Arbus's hate is harder to see in the pictures. It's more to do with the gaze, the process of composition, the flaws she put front and center by ambushing her subject's interior. Plath made hate a subject. That was the solution she landed on, partly by reading Freud: His essay "Mourning and Melancholia" focused on depression, loss, anger, and suicide. The essay is complex, and judging from Plath's journal notes about it, there were portions she misunderstood. But one idea in particular she accurately absorbed: Freud's prescription for dealing with hate. Unless it exhausts itself by finding appropriate objects, it revolves upon the self. Plath took this thought deadly seriously. The objects were easy to find—father and mother. Her poems buried them both; she hated them dead. Apparently, though, there was hate left over, too much to go around. It didn't help that Plath romanticized suicide. Her loving devotion to its lure, its siren call, was tinged with the erotic. Some argue Plath, like Arbus, never intended to die. She expected, perhaps like Arbus, to be found and restored. Of course, in Plath's case there was a precedent. She had been saved before. She had come close without succeeding. Coming close was an "art," she said; something she did "exceptionally well." In the end, she was *too* good at it.

The list of creative people who suicide is long. This isn't the place to attempt a survey. Plenty of uncreative people suicide, too, leaving no art behind to sift through. But there's a different, less actuarial question to ask. What about artists whose work *is* the demonic—an inner chaotic wound—who dedicate themselves to its description? Is there a sense in which art kills? Not on its own, but in combination with other factors?

I think so. Plath is a prototype case. She couldn't survive her subject matter. She'd been depressed before, suicidal too, but the last set of poems, those written in the final six months of her life, virtually required a death. It was the same for Kurt Cobain, who started building his own suicide myth early on. He was never going to fade away. His songs, so uncanny, impossibly dark—full of references to guns, dying, self-hate, enemies— traced a black circuit. Suffering was his mode; it was what he did, endlessly. The songs catalogued the ways it came about, the hows, the whys. The songs, in other words, intensified the feel- ings. They were an exacerbation. The songs were an *accelerant.*

This is art in general. *It's an accelerant.* It renews the intensity of the feelings on display—the facts, the images, the shards of life history. It quickens the pace. Art is also a baring. It can make things harder, not easier. It's a visible ugly proof, not a transmog- rification. If the theme is suffering, then art's more suffering. It has to be to succeed. The writer Kathryn Harrison wrote a scandalous memoir, *The Kiss,* about her consensual affair with her own father when she was nineteen. It's hard to imagine a subject more taboo. Incest books aren't especially uncommon, but they typically adopt an abuse perspective. There are incest *victims,* incest *survivors.* Harrison takes a different line, far braver, far more dangerous. There is no assignment of blame. No evil culprit, no victim. It's the opposite of a soothing simplification. And getting to this place, the pain's location—the art's location, too, when the art *is* the pain—is anything but easy. "I know when I was writing *The Kiss* I was emotionally closer to the material than I had been while experiencing it," Harrison told me. "The defenses I'd used in the moment—and they were whatever I could muster—were what I had to strip away, deliberately, in order to write honestly. And I was more grief- stricken, and angry, and appalled, and any number of other things, than I had been when actually involved with my father."[4] There are two things to notice here. First, the art is *more* painful than the experience it's based on. In certain instances, as with Harrison's, the return entails intensification, acceleration. Art is not a cooling, it's a heating up. There's little self-therapy going on. And the reason why concerns the stripping away, Harrison's second revelation. Making the art—or, more to the point, making it good, honest, powerful—demands a lowering of defenses. What gets one through the experience initially must be given up, cleared away in order to see plainly. The function of defense is negotiated, disguised happiness. Defenses transform feeling, reroute it away from its source. To get where it sometimes needs to go, art has to be *defenseless*. "Happiness," as Philip Larkin observed with his usual acidity, "writes white." Writing dark requires a relinquishing. There is no light. One goes into the dark darkly. It's the only true way to see it.

Unlike Arbus or Plath or Cobain, Harrison survived the descent. But writing *The Kiss* required risking not surviving. For Plath, writing *Ariel* risked the same thing, as did Arbus's "graven" images (in Howard's words), Cobain's death-drenched songs, Jung's theorizing. Still, as Harrison explains, "There's a part of me who feels that death is the only answer to incest. The only way to remove the pollution."[5] It's as if a price has to be paid. The pollution's just that—polluting. The dark art darkens the life that made it. One has to live with what deliberate defenselessness dredges up—by making more art, perhaps, or absorbing what the art made necessary—or not. *Pollution* is an interesting word. It's similar to the words Arbus used—*dirty, perverse*. Once this dirtiness gets raised, it becomes a problem. There is no shield. It's right there, irrepressible, inescapable. I talked about this dilemma already. It's one Arbus never solved, at least not successfully. She tried splitting, keeping the dark separate, sequestering it in split images—the good twin, the evil twin. But splitting's a defense, a short-term measure. Set apart, the fragment sharpens like a rogue nation. Boxed away, it gathers strength. The tough job, as Jung tried outlining, is letting it in once it's out, making a place for it, colonizing it. It needs to be absorbed, somehow, into the total working personality. But when the dark is as dark as it was for Arbus, and for similar artists, absorption's destructive potential is high. Letting it in is a risk. The dark paints the daytime black. And from there it's all black, all the time.

A lot of artists go dark in order to create; if that leaves their lives hard to live in, hard to step back into after the descent is made, the art benefits proportionally. In fact, another thing Arbus and Plath had in common was this: Both believed they were doing their very best work in their final months. For Arbus, it was the photographs of the mentally retarded; for Plath, it was the *Ariel* poems. In Plath's case, there was no equivocation, no doubt. She knew for certain that her last poems were vastly superior to anything else she had ever done before. She knew they were genius-level achievements. She knew there had been a breakthrough. Arbus entertained a bit more doubt. Her opinion vacillated. On one hand, the shots of the mentally retarded were what she'd always been aiming for in her work, a new beginning, a fresh development; on the other, she began to wonder, in the last weeks of her life, whether the shots were "doing" what she wanted them to. There was love and hate. The same splitting typical of Arbus in general.

AN EMERGENCY IN SLOW MOTION

Doon Arbus is less ambivalent than her mother. She believes Diane recognized in these pictures "something new, something she'd been searching for for a long time." The discovery, Doon says, "set [Diane] free." Making the shots entailed "giving up certain elements of style and technique," according to Doon. Precision was surrendered for lyricism, irony for emotional purity, "authority for tenderness." Arbus before had always been, Doon says, the "invisible center" of her pictures; now she was subsumed. The collaborator became "a witness." The result, in Doon Arbus's view, is Diane's most transcendent, romantic, revelatory work, each image a metaphor, a riddle "without words or answers," a fragment of "an unwritten fairy tale."[6]

Arbus did blur in the shots of the mentally retarded; there was no collaboration. And this is a massive shift, nearly a new style. But Arbus came to realize she got nothing back from these pictures. There was no mirroring of the sort one sees clearly in so many of the earlier images, no projection of personal trauma, no subjective infiltration. Diane Arbus—the presence, Doon says, "you couldn't see and couldn't ignore" in the freaks and sex shots—"goes all but unnoticed." This is what constitutes the work's discontinuity. Arbus disappeared. Her life stopped being the subtext. "She knew the value of what she was giving up," Doon maintains, "and the value of what she was gaining in return."[7]

Doon Arbus has become Diane's posthumous interpreter; Ted Hughes was Sylvia's, in his occasional forewords to the work and his book of poems, *Birthday Letters*, a virtual poetical psycho-biography of his wife. Hughes says about the *Ariel* poems the same thing Doon says about the shots of the mentally retarded.

They set Sylvia free; they were a jailbreak. And they represented her true self, the one all the prior work shackled in its formality and ornateness, its surfacy accomplishment.

So in their last months both Arbus and Plath sought the revelatory. Each evolved a new style, each was set free by this evolution, each made art of a different order entirely. It was the best they could do. It was an apex. It was a beginning. Then it was an end.

But the end came for different reasons. Achieving masterpiece work draws incredibly deeply on the creator. For one thing, it's enormously difficult. It's a constant tension, a strain, an agitation. It's depleting—it has to be—and then when it's over, there's the refilling, which doesn't always come quickly, if ever. Also, when you reach the top, realize the art's potential to its fullest, the second act is daunting. There's no topping the top. Truman Capote is an example. *In Cold Blood* almost killed him to write—literally. It was named (by most) a masterpiece. Then nothing more came. He threatened the book *Answered Prayers*, a skewering of social elites in whose orbit he futilely loitered, but it never arrived. His energy spent, there was to be no resuscitation. And he knew what it took to bring a masterpiece off. He doubted he had the necessary emotional, imaginative, or literary leftovers.[8]

Where Plath and Arbus differ is in the use made of self. Plath exhumed a buried voice and it spoke scorchingly, with saved-up force. It was truer, more her, but it was a live wire she grabbed on to, and it killed her. She foreclosed on the demon. Arbus, in the shots of the mentally retarded, stepped out of the subjective for the first time. The self evaporated. And for someone whose hold on identity was never particularly sure to begin with, the evaporation left an abyss. It may have been thrilling to begin with, it may have seemed like what she was always after, but in the end erasure was hard to accept. She didn't exist in the work anymore, and if she didn't exist in the work, she didn't exist. The key to Arbus's suicide was Marvin Israel, the difficulties in their relationship, his failure to be what she wanted and needed, his turning away. The art added insult to injury. He wasn't doing it for her anymore. The art wasn't either. He was erasing her; the art was self-erasure. These two developments combined to make a lot of nothing. This "foreign country," to use Doon Arbus's words again, was a different kind of shantytown. All the squatters were gone. There was no governess to go in with and no governess to guide her back out. Also, the mentally retarded kept no secrets to swap. The mutual confessing stopped. As Doon Arbus wrote, "these photographs simply disclose themselves." They state, "this is how it is."[9] But in their silence and stillness, they bring us "face to face with stuff we feel we weren't meant to know." I don't think Arbus wanted to know it either—what these shots said about why she photographed. But she had to. The shots required it. She made them, and they unmade her.

ACKNOWLEDGMENTS

This book was a long time in the making and there are several people I need to thank. It was my wife, Theresa Love, a writer herself, who first suggested Arbus to me as a person I might investigate. At the time I had no idea that suggestion would lead to this book. But it did, and I am enormously grateful. One fateful day elements miraculously aligned, and I met my agent, Betsy Lerner, who then changed my life (though she humbly denies this). Besides being an agent, Betsy is a writer—an outstanding writer—and she provided pages of editorial comment on the book. She is sui generis. I can't thank her enough. My editor at Bloomsbury is Kathy Belden, whom I adored from our very first phone conversation and never stopped adoring. Kathy also sharpened the book immeasurably. Her comments on chapters were clear, direct, and wise. I'd also like to thank the copyeditor, Will Georgantas, and the production editor, Nathaniel Knaebel.

Then there are the people who lent a hand in assorted ways, with dust-jacket design, permissions, and interviews. These include Dr. Helen Boigon; Seth Boigon; Phyllis and Eberhard Kronhausen; Margaret "Peggy" Nemerov; Kathryn Harrison; Margit Erb; the library staff at Washington University in St. Louis; and hundreds of students, doctoral and undergraduate, who listened to what I had to say about Arbus even when what I had to say amounted to very little.

A NOTE ON SOURCES

The two books I rely on most in my interpretation of Arbus's psychological life and the subjective origins of her photographic work are Patricia Bosworth's 1984 study, *Diane Arbus: A Biography*, and the Arbus estate's 2003 *Revelations*. These titles are must-reads for anyone interested in the facts of Arbus's interior world, her sense of herself and her art. Other sources include Arbus's two childhood autobiographies written as class assignments and housed in the Howard Nemerov Papers at Washington University in St. Louis, as well as the introduction to the posthumous book *Diane Arbus*, which contains various Arbus comments "edited from tape recordings of a series of classes" along with interviews and writings.

My interviews with Arbus's psychotherapist Helen Boigon occurred throughout the winter of 2005. We talked on the phone several times, and Boigon also mailed me a long handwritten letter along with a paper she had written on art and creativity.

The interview with the Kronhausens, conducted over e-mail, is from December of 2007.

NOTES

INTRODUCTION

1. See William J. McGuire, "Creative Hypothesis Generating in Psychology: Some Useful Heuristics," *Annual Review of Psychology* 48 (1997): 1–30.
2. Vladimir Nabokov, *Lectures on Literature* (New York: Harcourt Brace Jovanovich, 1980).
3. Diane Arbus, *Diane Arbus: An Aperture Monograph* (New York: Aperture, 1972), 15.
4. Ibid., 5.

Chapter 1: ESSENTIAL MYSTERIES

1. Arbus, *Aperture,* 8.
2. Diane Arbus, *Revelations* (New York: Random House, 2003), 203.
3. Patricia Bosworth, *Diane Arbus: A Biography* (New York: Norton, 1984), 319.
4. Arbus, *Revelations,* 225, and Bosworth, 318–321.
5. J. Malcolm, "Good Pictures," *New York Review of Books* (January 15, 2004): 4–7.
6. Arbus, *Revelations,* 144.
7. Ibid., 147.

8. Ibid.

9. Ibid., 146.

10. Arbus, *Aperture*, 1.

11. Arbus, *Revelations*, 156.

12. Ibid., 157.

13. Ibid., 196.

14. The text of "The Full Circle," along with photographs, is reproduced in Doon Arbus and Marvin Israel, eds., *Diane Arbus: Magazine Work* (New York: Aperture, 1984), 14–23.

15. Arbus, *Revelations*, 160.

16. Ibid., 159.

17. Ibid., 163.

18. Ibid., 190.

19. Ibid., 195.

20. Ibid., 198.

21. Ibid., 200.

22. Ibid., 197.

23. Helen Boigon interview, winter 2005. All quoted statements from Boigon are derived from interviews I conducted with her in 2005. Also in 2005 she mailed me a long handwritten letter in which she described the therapy with Arbus and her impressions of her as a person, artist, and client.

24. Arbus, *Aperture*, 1.

25. Ibid.

26. Bosworth, 318.

27. Lisette Model interview, http://epnweb.org/index.php.

28. Reprinted in Arbus, *Revelations*, 219.

Chapter 2: THE SECRET

1. See Howard Nemerov, *Journal of the Fictive Life* (New York: Rutgers University Press, 1965).

2. "Interview with Renee Nemerov Brown, Diane Arbus's Sister,"

American Suburb X, http://www.americansuburbx.com/2009/01/theory-interview-with-renee-nemerov.html.

3. Both of these autobiographies are part of the Howard Nemerov Papers, housed at Washington University in St. Louis.

4. Bosworth, 278–279.

5. Helmut Newton is a photographer with a history similar to Arbus's in the sense that he was raised in a wealthy family; brought up by "Kinderfrauleins" and a nervous, frequently nap-taking mother who "didn't give a shit whether I froze to death with my purse in the park or not"; and shuttled around in chauffeur-driven vehicles. Those facts make it especially intriguing that he recalls, in his autobiography, an episode quite like Arbus's: "There was a *terrain vague* opposite the apartment building where I was born, and sometimes in the summer a little circus or sideshow would pull up there. I used to look out the window and beg my Kinderfraulein to take me down there and let me walk through the booths and look at the fat woman and the sideshows. There was something forbidden about it. I would have to be home by seven. There weren't many freaks, although there were people who showed themselves for money." In this case, Newton was allowed to descend, also with his governess. See Helmut Newton, *Autobiography* (New York: Random House, 2003).

6. Renee Nemerov interview.

7. Arbus, *Revelations*, 124.

8. Ibid., 124.

9. For a review of these attachment-related research findings, see P. Shaver and M. Mikulincer, "Attachment-Related Psychodynamics," *Attachment and Human Development* 4 (2002): 133–161.

10. Renee Nemerov interview.

11. Bosworth, 9.

12. Ibid., 25.

13. Ibid., 27.

14. Renee Nemerov interview.
15. Bosworth, 19.
16. Ibid., 36.
17. Ibid., 37.
18. Ibid.
19. Ibid., 278.
20. Ibid., 11.
21. Renée Nemerov interview.
22. Bosworth, 12.
23. Howard Nemerov, 75.
24. Ibid., 74.
25. Ibid., 75.
26. Ibid., 77.
27. Ibid., 75.
28. Ibid., 77.
29. Ibid.
30. Ibid., 79.
31. Arbus, *Revelations*, 124.
32. Howard Nemerov, 80.
33. Ibid., 82.
34. Ibid.
35. Ibid.
36. Ibid., 84.
37. Arbus, *Aperture*, 2.
38. L. France, "A rare interview with Penelope Tree, the Ultimate Sixties It Girl," *The Observer* (August 3, 2008).
39. Ibid.
40. Ibid.
41. The shot of eleven-year-old Marcella Matthaei, taken in December 1969, captures the same adolescent fury, except Tree appears invulnerable while Marcella might dissolve into tears. Matthaei recalls: "I was on my way to a party . . . Sitting around with a stranger taking pictures of me was the last thing on my

mind. What you see on my face is, 'Get this over and done with. My mom and dad told me to do this.'" See D. Segal, "Double Exposure: A Moment with Diane Arbus Created a Lasting Impression," *Washington Post* (May 12, 2005).

42. Arbus, *Revelations*, 191.
43. See G. Clarke, *The Photograph* (New York: Oxford University Press, 1997).
44. For a wide-ranging review of attachment-related findings, see J. Cassidy and P. Shaver, *Handbook of Attachment, Second Edition* (New York: Guilford Press, 2008).

Chapter 3: FAIRY TALES FOR GROWN-UPS

1. Bosworth, 34.
2. Arbus, *Aperture*, 5–6.
3. Arbus, *Revelations*, 128.
4. Ibid.
5. Ibid.
6. Bosworth, 34.
7. Ibid.
8. Ibid., 39.
9. Ibid., 44.
10. Ibid., 34.
11. Ibid., 35.
12. Ibid.
13. Ibid., 40.
14. Ibid., 41.
15. Ibid., 46.
16. Ibid., 53.
17. Arbus, *Revelations*, 131.
18. Ibid., 130.
19. Ibid.
20. Bosworth, 59.

21. Arbus, *Revelations*, 131.

22. Diane Arbus lecture, formerly at http://www.almanacmagazine .com/april/arbus.html. Initially, this Web site uploaded the actual audio recording of a lecture Arbus had given to a group of students in the spring of 1970. But as the site explains now, "Audio has been temporally taken down as a response and courtesy to an inquiry by the Arbus estate." This temporary response and courtesy has been in place, now, for more than a year.

23. "Jack Dracula on Diane Arbus," http://www.youtube.com.

24. Arbus and Israel,156.

25. Arbus, *Revelations*, 160.

26. Ibid., 156–157.

27. Diane Arbus lecture.

28. Ibid.

29. See, for more on Arbus's prototypical shantytown scene, William Todd Schultz, *Handbook of Psychobiography* (New York: Oxford University Press, 2005), 42–63.

30. Arbus, *Revelations*, 176.

31. Diane Arbus lecture.

32. Ibid.

33. Arbus, *Revelations*, 201.

34. Bosworth, 47.

35. Ibid., 82.

36. Ibid.

37. Ibid.

38. Ibid., 83.

39. Ibid., 84.

40. Ibid., 153.

41. Ibid.

42. Arbus, *Revelations*, 144.

43. Ann Thomas, *Lisette Model* (National Gallery of Canada: Ottowa, 1990). See chapter nine for an analysis of the Arbus/ Model relationship.

44. Thomas, 29.
45. Ibid., 30.
46. Ibid., 31.
47. Ibid., 34–35, 66.
48. Ibid., 99.
49. Ibid., 23.
50. Arbus and Israel, 14.
51. Ibid., 157.
52. Thomas, 78.
53. Ibid., 100.
54. Ibid., 95.
55. Ibid., 113.
56. Ibid.
57. Lisette Model interview.
58. Shelley Rice, "Essential Differences: A Comparison of the Portraits of Lisette Model and Diane Arbus," *Artforum* (1980): 66–72.
59. Rice, 67–68.
60. Ibid., 68.
61. Ibid., 69.
62. Ibid.
63. Ibid.
64. Ibid.
65. Ibid.
66. Ibid., 70.
67. Ibid. 71.
68. Hugh Hart, "For the Subject of Arbus' 'Child with a Toy Hand Grenade,' Life Was Forever Altered at the Click of a Shutter," *San Francisco Chronicle* (October 19, 2003).
69. "The Jewish Giant," interview with Milton Levine and Irwin Sherman. First aired on *All Things Considered*, National Public Radio, October 6, 1999. Transcript available at http://www .soundportraits.org/on-air/the_jewish_giant/transcript.php.

70. Arbus, *Revelations*, 190.

71. Bosworth, 194.

72. Arbus, *Aperture*, 14–15.

73. Arbus and Israel, 20.

74. Ibid., 20.

75. Ibid., 17.

76. Ibid., 20.

77. Ibid.

78. Ibid., 23.

79. Ibid.

80. Arbus, *Revelations*, 159.

81. Bosworth, 217.

82. Arbus, *Revelations*, 182.

83. Ibid.

84. Renee Nemerov interview.

85. David Siegel, "Double Exposure: A Moment with Diane Arbus Created a Lasting Impression," *Washington Post* (May 12, 2005).

86. Arbus and Israel, 169.

87. R.D. Laing, *The Divided Self: An Existential Study in Sanity and Madness* (New York: Routledge, 2000; first published in 1964), 195.

88. Ibid., 189–190.

89. Ibid., 59.

90. Ibid.

91. Ibid., 120–121.

92. Ibid., 124.

93. Bosworth, 11.

94. Ibid., 25.

95. Laing, 54.

96. Ibid.

97. Ibid., 56.

98. Ibid., 197.

99. See, for a summary of these ideas, Schultz, *Handbook of Psycho-biography*, 126–127.
100. Arbus, *Aperture*, 2.
101. Bosworth, 180.

Chapter 4: SHAME ERASING

1. Arbus, *Revelations*, 166.
2. Ibid., 166–167.
3. Ibid., 167.
4. Ibid., 177.
5. Ibid., 152.
6. Greer's comments in this section are from Bosworth, 314–315.
7. Arbus, *Revelations*, 220.
8. Ibid., 178.
9. Ibid.
10. Ibid.
11. Ibid., 180.
12. All comments in this section from the Kronhausens are taken from an interview conducted by e-mail in April 2005.
13. Arbus, *Aperture*, 3.
14. Ibid., 12.
15. Ibid., 15.
16. Ibid.
17. Arbus, *Revelations*, 179.
18. For Arbus's thoughts on nudism—now referred to as naturism—see Arbus and Israel, 68–69.
19. Arbus, *Revelations*, 174.
20. Ibid., 4.
21. Sources for this section on "openness" and the various relationships between it and other personality characteristics include the following:
    Robert McCrae and Paul Costa, "The Five Factor Theory of

Personality," in *Handbook of Personality: Theory and Research*, edited by Oliver John, Richard Robins, and Lawrence Pervin (New York: Guilford Press, 2008), 159–181.

David Watson and Lee Anna Clark, "Extraversion and Its Positive Emotional Core," and Robert McCrae and Paul Costa, "Conceptions and Correlates of Openness to Experience," in *Handbook of Personality Psychology*, edited by Robert Hogan, John Johnson, and Stephen Briggs (San Diego: Academic Press, 1997).

22. See, for findings on sex and attachment style, D. Davis, P. Shaver, and M. Vernon, "Attachment Style and Subjective Motivations for Sex," *Personality and Social Psychology Bulletin* 30 (2004): 1076–1090.

23. The seminal article on correlations between openness and depression is Miriam Wolfenstein and Timothy Trull, "Depression and Openness to Experience," *Journal of Personality Assessment* 69 (1997): 614–632.

24. Arbus, *Aperture*, 14–15.

Chapter 5: THE BLACK KNOT

1. Arbus, *Revelations*, 143.

2. Ibid., 208.

3. Ibid., 190.

4. Ibid., 189.

5. Ibid., 190.

6. Bosworth, 269.

7. Helen Boigon interview.

8. Arbus, *Revelations*, 207–208.

9. Ibid., 216.

10. "Diane Arbus Revisited," *Black & White*, April 2005, Issue 36, 48.

11. Arbus, *Revelations*, 144.

12. Ibid., 217.

Chapter 6: SWEEPING BACK THE OCEAN

1. Arbus, *Revelations,* 225.

2. See M. Heiman, "Psychoanalytic Observations on the Last Painting and Suicide of Vincent van Gogh," *International Journal of Psychoanalysis* 57 (1976): 71–84.

3. See C. Hammen and P. Brennan, "Depressed Adolescents of Depressed and Nondepressed Mothers: Tests of an Interpersonal Impairment Hypothesis," *Journal of Consulting and Clinical Psychology* 69 (2001): 284–294.

4. See M. Mikulincer and P. Shaver, *Attachment in Adulthood: Structure, Dynamics, and Change* (New York: Guilford Press, 2007).

5. Bosworth, 246–247.

6. Ibid., 206.

7. Ibid., 256.

8. Ibid., 302.

9. Ibid., 276.

10. Ibid., 276–277.

11. Ibid., 267.

12. Ibid., 269.

13. Arbus, *Revelations,* 194.

14. Ibid., 193–194.

15. Bosworth, 272.

16. Ibid., 278.

17. Arbus, *Revelations,* 212.

18. Bosworth, 283.

19. Ibid., 285

20. Ibid., 286.

21. Ibid., 290.

22. Arbus, *Revelations,* 215.

23. Ibid., 217.

24. Ibid., 219.

25. Ibid., 221.

26. Ibid., 215.

27. Bosworth, 312.

28. Ibid., 315.

29. Ibid.

30. Arbus, *Revelations*, 223.

31. Bosworth, 319.

32. Arbus, *Revelations*, 225.

33. For a summary of suicide risk factors, see K.R. Jamison, *Night Falls Fast: Understanding Suicide* (New York: Vintage, 1990).

34. Arbus, *Revelations*, 224.

35. Ibid., 224.

36. Bosworth, 282.

37. Ibid., 263.

38. Ibid.

39. Arbus, *Revelations*, 190.

40. Bosworth, 262.

41. Germaine Greer, "Wrestling with Diane Arbus," *The Guardian* (October 8, 2005).

42. Arbus, *Revelations*, 204.

43. Ibid., 221.

44. T. Joiner, "The Psychology and Neurobiology of Suicidal Behavior," *Annual Review of Psychology* 54 (2005): 287–314.

45. Arbus, *Revelations*, 225.

46. Ibid.

47. Bosworth, 313.

48. Because this class of drug is not used as widely today, most of the research on barbiturate poisoning is relatively old. See Edward Whiting, O. Barrett, and T. Inmon, "Treatment of Barbiturate Poisoning," *California Medicine* 102 (1964): 367–369. Also, R. Crone, D.E. Johnson, and E. Anderson, "Acute Barbiturate Intoxication: A Case of Extremely High Content on the Blood and Protracted Coma with Recovery," *California*

Medicine 88 (1958): 166–169. Further information may be found at http://emedicine.medscape.com/article/813155-overview.

49. Statistics on suicide may be found in abundance at suicide.org, a nonprofit organization and Web site.

Chapter 7: THE HOLE IN THE GROUND WHERE SECRETS LIVED

1. See, for example, Alan Elms, *Uncovering Lives* (New York: Oxford University Press, 1993).
2. See my analysis of Plath in the *Handbook of Psychobiography.*
3. C.G. Jung, *Memories, Dreams, Reflections* (New York: Vintage, 1989; first published in 1963).
4. Personal communication with Kathryn Harrison, March 2010.
5. Ibid.
6. See Diane Arbus, *Untitled* (New York: Aperture, 2005).
7. Ibid.
8. See William Todd Schultz, *Tiny Terror: Why Truman Capote (Almost) Wrote* Answered Prayers (New York: Oxford University Press, 2011).
9. Arbus, *Untitled.*

INDEX

absorption (engulfment), 105, 213
aesthetics, and openness, 138, 139
agitation, 54
Ainsworth, Mary, 59
Alvarez, A., 170
ambiguity, 167–68
American Institute of Psychoanalysis, 147
Amis, Martin, 117, 201
Aperture Monograph, 100
Arbus, Allan (husband):
in the Army, 73
and Bosworth's biography, 13
and control, 71
and Diane's attachment, 6, 63,
70–71, 77, 85, 182
and Diane's death, 26
jobs of, 69
and marriage, 72, 73
and money matters, 140
move to California, 144–45,
159, 177, 190, 191
and photography, 73, 74–75, 81,
85, 86, 87
and secrets, 70, 162
separation and divorce, 84, 85,
144, 177, 182
theater work of, 85
Arbus, Amy (daughter), 26, 85,
111, 142, 143, 181, 198

Arbus, Diane:
and antidepressants, 174–75,
177, 183–84
and attachment, *see* attachment
autobiographies, *see* Arbus,
Diane, writings of
biography of, *see* Bosworth,
Patricia
birth of, 32–33
childhood of, 33, 34, 39–46,
47–49, 87, 93, 104
children of, *see* Arbus, Amy;
Arbus, Doon
conscience of, 37
depression of, 26, 43, 46, 96,
135, 138–39, 144, 145, 153–54,
162, 165, 171–76, 180, 181,
183–84, 190–91
dreams of, 28–29, 34–35,
175–76, 179, 191–92, 193
experience sought by, 136–37,
159, 190
family of, *see* Nemerov entries
and fear, 41, 184, 190
firsts of, 39
Guggenheim application of, 16
hepatitis of, 143–44, 175, 176, 181
as high "Openness" type,
134–39, 157, 159, 164–65, 192,
205–6

INDEX

Arbus, Diane, writings of, 13
 adolescent autobiography (1938),
  33, 35–38, 40–42, 43, 141,
  142, 161, 171, 183, 202
 appointment books, 15, 195, 196
 childhood autobiography (1934),
  14, 28, 33–35, 54
 "The Full Circle," 18, 21, 78,
  87–88, 92, 97–98
 "Last Supper," 194–96
 letters, 14
 negative emotions expressed in,
  54
 notebooks, 14, 15, 78, 83, 192
Arbus, Doon (daughter), 6, 142
 birth of, 73–74
 and Bosworth's biography, 13
 childhood of, 85
 double exposure of, 98, 101
 and mother's death, 26
 mother's letters to, 18
 and mother's work, 20, 170,
  214, 216
 in Paris, 181
 at Reed College, 111, 129
Arbus estate:
 approach to biography by, 4
 and Arbus's suicide, 166, 167,
  182, 195, 199
 and Bosworth's biography, 15
 material controlled by, 15, 91
 Revelations, 2, 14–15, 22, 50–51,
  84, 101, 121, 129, 166, 199
art:
 as accelerant, 211
 acting out via, 40, 80, 171
 as affect-driven, 172
 as autobiography, 5, 102, 173
 defensiveness in, 5
 digging into the origins of, 8,
  32, 136–37
 expectations in, 139

functions of, 172, 183, 211
 as mystery, 2, 205
 and pain, 212
 and personality, 6, 139
 secrets in, 52–53
 as self, 12, 111, 127, 173
 and self-erasure, 216
 and self-expression, 27, 108
 and self-mastery, 209
 theory into practice in, 119
 as therapy, 203
 and truth, 127–28
 as waking dream, 203
 will to work in, 150, 178
Artforum, 28–29, 90, 179
Art in America (Leffingwell), 160
artists:
 art separated from life by, 91
 boundaries trespassed by, 82
 and creativity, 139, 164–65, 185,
  203, 213
 and depression, 139, 183–84
 flaws seen by, 104
 obsessions of, 96, 150, 183
 personality dimensions of,
  134–39
 and rage, 184–85
 remaking themselves, 96
 as sexualized beings, 23–24
 as suicides, 27, 168–71, 183,
  210–11
attachment:
 affectional, 59
 and anger, 172
 anxious, 61, 62–63, 138, 139,
  153, 163, 172, 188
 and availability, 60
 avoidant, 61
 biographical approach based on,
  6, 54, 59–64
 characteristic adaptations of,
  63–64

psychotherapy (*continued*)
  art as, 203
  confrontations avoided in, 147
  empathy in, 151
  issues in Arbus's focus, 145–46
  neo-Freudian, 145
  presenting problem in, 145
  rapport required in, 151–52
  reenactments in, 156
  resistance to, 151, 155
  and sex, 157–58
  theory and technique in, 151
  understanding continuities in,
    146–47
  see also Boigon, Helen

Rational Emotive Behavior
    therapy (REBT), 119
Ratoucheff, Andrew, 17, 88
reactivity, 139
Revelations (Arbus estate), 2, 14–15,
    22, 50–51, 84, 101, 121, 129,
    166, 199
Rice, Shelley, 90–91, 93, 96, 204
RMS *Aquitania,* 34
Russek, Frank, 41
Russek's, 41, 44, 46–47, 69, 71
  photography assignments for,
    73, 74

saliency units, 43
Sammy's Bowery Follies, 88
schizophrenia, 105–9, 162–65,
    204
  and antidepressants, 174–75
  and Cluster C disorder, 164
  and relationships, 192–93
  and splitting, 213
Schneidman, Edwin, 188
Scott (chauffeur), 44
secondary process thinking,
    135

secrets, 202–6
  and art, 52–53
  and autobiography, 35–38
  and childhood, 52
  and confession, 25, 67, 173,
    202–3
  and masks, 21, 75
  modern obsession with, 113
  in parallel universes, 209
  sharing, 25, 113
  sick, 58
  uncovering, 25, 32, 36, 52, 54,
    80, 87, 122, 126, 128, 132, 133,
    163, 164, 205–6, 215
  in writing, 52
self-reliance, 62
sensitivity, 139
Seventeen, 74, 159
sex:
  Arbus's experiences of, 23, 67,
    173–74
  Arbus's interest in, 8, 21–24,
    112–13, 118–29, 130, 133–34,
    137, 162, 163, 190–91
  and attachment, 50, 137–38
  and free love, 122
  and guilt, 67, 71, 133
  Kronhausen (erotologists), 23
  manipulation in, 138, 157
  masturbation, 71–72, 119
  orgies, 67, 120, 126, 127, 173,
    174
  and poetry, 24
  pornographic movie, 23
  and protectiveness, 138
  and psychotherapy, 157–58
  risky, 138
  and sexualization, 78, 113
  with strangers, 23, 67, 133–34,
    138, 159, 173, 176, 190–91
  and suicide, 182
Shainberg, Larry, 196

A NOTE ON THE AUTHOR

WILLIAM TODD SCHULTZ has a Ph.D. in psychology and is a professor at Pacific University in Oregon, focusing on personality research and psychobiography. He edited and contributed to the groundbreaking *Handbook of Psychobiography*, and curates the book series Inner Lives, analyses of significant artists and political figures. His own book in the series, *Tiny Terror*, examines the life of Truman Capote. Schultz blogs for *Psychology Today* about the intersection of madness and creativity. His personal blog can be found at williamtoddschultz.wordpress.com.